I Will Not Leave You Orphans

You Orphans

The Story
of One Humble Servant
of God

Jenny L. Sheetz, MA, CN

Published by

WORDS THAT HEAL

A division of St. Joseph Institute, Inc.

ISBN 0-9769582-0-1

LCCN: 2005909707

Printed in the United States by Morris Publishing
3212 East Highway 30
Kearney, NE 68847
1-800-650-7888

Dedication

To the Sacred Heart of Jesus,
May You be known, loved and imitated.

Completed on March 15, 2005
The final day of the novena to the Sacred Heart of Jesus
in a year devoted to the Holy Eucharist.

Author's Note

I felt called by God to tell my story, and I believe His grace guided the process. Portions of the story could have been filled with horror and violence. However, I have no desire to inflict that type of pain on others, nor do I want to perpetuate the horror and violence to which I was subjected. My desire is to share the healing I received through my relationship with God. There is much that was left unsaid. What is important has been stated in the chapters that follow. Each of the chapters in Part I is titled with one or two verses of a prayer I say daily after receiving communion:

Anima Christi

Soul of Christ, sanctify me.
Body of Christ, save me.
Blood of Christ, inebriate me.
Water flowing from the side of Christ, wash me.
Passion of Christ, strengthen me.
O good Jesus, hear me.
Hide me within Your wounds.
Never permit me to be separated from You.
From the malignant enemy, defend me.
At the hour of my death, call me.
And bid me come to You,
That with Your Saints, I may praise You.
For everlasting ages. Amen.

Certain other prayers and concepts that are mentioned throughout the book may be found in an Appendix that follows the last chapter.

My life has been difficult. Often the support I needed was not available to me from those in this world who could have offered it. However, Jesus was always there for me. Jesus promised: "I will not leave you orphans; I will come to you" (Jn. 14:18). He fulfilled that promise for me many times over. My hope is that by reading this book you will realize how He has fulfilled that same promise for you.

May God bless you with the peace of Christ,

Jenny

Table of Contents

Part 1

Finding healing through my relationship with God.

Brothers and sisters: You were once in darkness, but now you are light in the Lord. Live as children of light, for light produces every kind of goodness and righteousness and truth. Try to learn what is pleasing to the Lord. Take no part in the fruitless works of darkness; rather expose them, for it is shameful even to mention the things done by them in secret; but everything exposed by the light becomes visible, for everything that becomes visible is light. Therefore, it says: "Awake, O sleeper, and arise from the dead, and Christ will give you light." (Eph. 5: 8-14)

Note: *The information that is shared throughout this book is not intended to point fingers or blame others for their choices. The sole purpose is to share the reality that the impact of those choices created for me at the time they were made, as well as the consequences that followed later.*

1

The Journey Begins

Although I had been raised in the Christian faith, I had never known Jesus in the way I was about to know Him. I had no intellectual understanding of His Eucharistic Presence. For me, Jesus was an historical figure who was responsible for our salvation. He was a person who I would be fortunate to meet in heaven where He lived with God. He was not yet someone who was a conscious part of my daily life. He was distant – somewhere in the past or somewhere in the future. I only knew *about* Him. I did not *know* Him. All of this was about to change.

In my early 30's I married a man who was Catholic and had three young sons. In an effort to be unified as a family, I chose to attend Mass with them each Sunday even though I was Protestant. Sunday after Sunday we sat in the first row in the balcony at St. Mary's – a church dedicated to the Immaculate Heart of Mary. Every Sunday I tried to sit, stand, and kneel at the proper time during Mass. The celebration of the Mass intrigued me. I listened attentively and watched with curiosity. However, I had no real understanding of the events that were taking place.

One morning while we were kneeling at the consecration I was captivated by a mysterious sight. First of all, I had no idea what the consecration was. All I knew was that we were supposed to kneel while the priest at the altar held up the bread and wine. Enthralled solely by the ritual,

I watched intently as the altar boy rang the bell when the priest elevated the host. What seemed like an ordinary event became quite extraordinary to me. The host appeared to be surrounded by flickering golden lights during the time the bell was ringing. I watched silently. Then to my great amazement the same golden lights surrounded the chalice filled with wine as it was elevated by the priest. Excitedly, I reached over and tugged at my husband's arm, exclaiming, "Did you *see* that!"

I could tell by the look on his face that he had not had the same vision. He looked quite puzzled and asked what I saw. After hearing my explanation, he told me Catholics believe that the bread and wine become the Body and Blood of Jesus at the consecration. Because of what I had just witnessed, I knew that had to be the truth. I sat spellbound by the wonder and awe of the moment. It was an overwhelming reality, and yet, it was just the beginning of my walk with Jesus. It was as if He appeared in that moment to introduce Himself to me, and let me know that He is alive in the present, as well as in the past and in the future.

I had this same experience at the moment of consecration for several weeks. It was as if Jesus wanted to be sure I got the message about His real presence in the Eucharist. I did get the message in part, but there was far more that He wanted me to understand. Knowing about the real presence of Jesus was only the beginning. His purpose for giving me that knowledge was to help me understand His desire to develop an intimate relationship with me. He knew that I was about to endure nine years of terror and torment as I recalled the horrific events of my childhood. These events were stored in my unconscious mind because I was unable to handle them when they occurred. One by one they would emerge into my conscious mind as the events of the present created doorways to knowledge of past events that had been too painful to consciously endure during my childhood. Jesus had been with me then, and He was committed to remaining with me throughout the periods of intense suffering that were to come.

For now, His purpose was to form a trusting relationship with me that would encourage me to learn to depend on Him. He knew that I had never had the good fortune to develop healthy dependence as a child. It was important for me to learn to depend on Him. To that end, He called out to me one day after Mass. I had stayed after Mass to simply sit quietly. I got up from the pew and began to walk toward the back of the church, when I heard the words, "Remain with Me." Thinking that there was no one in the church, I was confused by hearing these words. They were said clearly and distinctly as if someone had spoken them from the front of the church. I spun around to face the altar, only to find no one there. I paused, staring at the sanctuary. Again, I heard, "Remain with Me." This time I realized that the voice I had heard was coming from the tabernacle – the place where Jesus resides in the church.

Slowly and cautiously, I walked toward the front of the church. I entered the first pew on the right hand side and sat in front of the tabernacle. I said nothing, and He said nothing more. We remained together in silence for sometime, until I felt that I was free to go. This was my first intimate encounter with our Lord in the Blessed Sacrament. It was the beginning of a pattern that continues to this day – a pattern that has been a source of nourishment, support, discipline, wisdom, and infinite mercy.

2

Soul of Christ, Sanctify Me.

It was through the mercy of Christ that God sought and found me. I was a lost sheep that had wandered away from the fold. I harbored no hostility toward God, nor did I recklessly tempt God's love for me. I had simply strayed into the wilderness because God was absent from my daily life. I was like a lamb caught in the thicket and unable to move. I was blind to the abuse that had occurred in my childhood, and at the same time I was bound by those events. From a subconscious level they reached into my present and controlled my life. I needed to be set free, and yet, I was not strong enough to endure the process of discovery and healing. There was much to be revealed. My cross was enormous and burdensome. God knew that my healing could only come through knowing His Son in the passion and resurrection.

The Eucharistic Prayer for Masses of Reconciliation states:

> When we were lost and could not find the way
> to You, You loved us more than ever: Jesus, Your
> Son, innocent and without sin, gave Himself
> into our hands and was nailed to a cross.

Just as He came to the people of God collectively, Jesus came to me individually. He found me in the thicket, and began the process of setting me free. One by one He removed the branches that held me bound and lifted the veil that kept me blind. It was not an instantaneous process. Instead, it unfolded in God's time, according to His plan.

Before I could begin the journey that would heal my past, I had to grow in my faith. I had to learn to seek holiness. I needed Jesus, Shepherd of Souls, to sanctify my soul with His presence and infuse me with the desire to become holy. He worked toward that goal from many directions.

First of all, He came to me. He talked and I listened. He called me to attend daily Mass, even though I was not yet Catholic and would not convert to the faith for four more years. He insisted that I attend Mass daily at 7:00AM. When I protested, using my responsibilities as an excuse, His response was, "Get up earlier." Early in my walk with God I was somewhat more obstinate than I am now, and I remarked: "If you really want me to be here, you will wake me up each day. Then I will come to Mass." God became my *alarm clock*. Prior to this time I had not been "a morning person." However, from that moment forward I awoke each day bright and alert and ready to attend daily Mass.

I quickly grew to cherish my *appointments* with God every morning. During Mass, He instructed me through His word and taught me to love Him in the Eucharist. Each day He would highlight some aspect of the Mass – a quote from sacred Scripture, a line from one of the prayers, or a message in the homily offered by the priest. I always knew how He wanted me to focus my prayer time after Mass. It was as if the words He chose for my meditation appeared like flashing neon lights in my mind or in my heart. He taught me to ponder those words in my heart in imitation of Mary, the mother of Jesus. He taught me the power of reflection. By creating quiet places within me, He was able to plant seeds of wisdom from His word. These seeds took root immediately and began to grow. They produced fruit in many parts of my life.

These daily encounters with God began to strengthen my faith. I began to depend on Him to help me with other aspects of my life. I had been called to a practice in the healing arts as a result of finding relief from my own suffering through various types of bodywork. God became an integral part of my healing practice. Each work day began at Mass where I spent three hours with Jesus in the Blessed Sacrament before going to my office. Once I arrived in the office, I would pray that the work I would complete that day would be for the highest good of the souls concerned, according to the will and plan of God. At work I came to know Jesus as healer. I prayed to see with the eyes of God, hear with the ears of God, speak with the mouth of God, and touch with the hands of God. I prayed that my office would be filled with sacred space and the presence of Christ to facilitate healing for those God called to my care.

God inspired many people to seek healing through my hands and the gift of good counsel that He had given me. I allowed Him to work through me, constantly observing with wonder and awe the power of His grace. I often felt as though I received as much healing as the people who were touched by my hands. Because I would allow *myself* to decrease and *Christ* within me to increase, the flow of divine grace would bring light and healing on many levels – physically, mentally, emotionally, and spiritually. I developed total trust in the flow of God's grace. He was teaching me to depend on Him.

Dependence on God went beyond the healing sessions. He inspired me to pray for those who came to me for healing. I prayed each morning at Mass to create sacred space in my office. I invited the healing presence of Christ into every session, and I offered each person up to God through the mystery of the presentation of Christ in the temple. This pattern of healing became a way of life for me. It helped me focus on the power of God to bring forth healing, and it took the responsibility of the outcome off my shoulders. It prevented me from creating any illusions about *my ability to heal*, and it gave me the assurance that the power would not be abused in any way. It also eased the burden of pain and sadness that I carried with those who were suffering.

In addition to my daily prayers, God inspired me to walk the way of the cross with Jesus every Friday. He helped me understand that some burdens were simply too heavy to bear through daily prayer. Some suffering could only be healed through the power of the cross. Each Friday morning at Mass I would recall the suffering of those I had touched that week. After Mass I would offer their suffering up to God in union with the passion of Christ. I learned to pause at each station of the cross and truly *be with* Jesus in His suffering. He began to talk to me through the events of His passion. Through our conversations I came to understand the healing that is offered to us through the stations of the cross. I recorded these messages of healing and began to share them with my clients during their sessions and through the publication of my newsletter. In this sharing I witnessed further healing, and I came to understand the universal power of the messages.

God was teaching me through my experiences and through my relationships. He was helping me grow in holiness by allowing me to experience His love each day in my time of prayer and reflection. He then inspired me to take the love that I received from Him and offer it to others in my healing practice. Because God first loved me, I grew in my ability to love others.

I also grew in holiness through my dependence on God. It was as if He took me by the hand each day and showed me the path that lay before me. He offered guidance and support. He corrected me when I began to go astray. He was a perfect parental figure – patient, kind, and filled with wisdom. He taught me that I was His *delight*. He treated me always as a gift, and never as a burden. He reminded me of some very special people He had placed in my life during my childhood.

I believe that God wanted to imprint knowledge of the characteristics of His own identity on me during the early years of my life through my relationship with several important people. These people served as a life preserver to me, giving me strength throughout my childhood and powerful memories to anchor me in the reality of God's goodness. My great-grandfather, my great-aunt, and my uncle touched my young life with the goodness of God. They were a source of light in a time of great darkness. They spent time with me, teaching me to read, to cook, to pray, to sing, and to play. They brought balance into my life; they treated me as a gift; and they introduced me to God.

My great grandfather took me to church every Sunday where we sat behind my grandparents and their children – all except my dad who was too busy working to attend church. Attending Sunday school and church had been an important part of family life for generations, until my father became focused on a desire to succeed in business. Then nothing mattered, except *his* dream. Everything in our lives revolved around *his* drive to succeed. As a result, I learned to submit my life to the will of other people, instead of submitting to the will of God. By the time I was in third grade I stopped attending church and Sunday school because I was expected to work in the store on Sunday morning. The neighbors used to joke with my father about reporting him for violating the child labor laws. I was no longer a gift – no longer a child of God. Instead, I was a slave. I sacrificed my childhood to the creation of a chain of convenience stores. The sad reality is that there was no sense of appreciation for the sacrifice, no recognition for what I lost or for what I contributed.

Jesus entered my life to teach me that I was no longer a slave, but a friend. In fact, I realized that I was *more than a friend* of Jesus. He was an older brother to me because I was a child of God. This revelation was years in the making, and it was all part of God's plan for my life. Sometimes we learn about the goodness of God by directly experiencing that goodness. This was the experience I had with my great grandfather. Other times we learn about goodness, and the value it represents, because we have been deprived of it for sometime. Then through the grace to re-experience and reclaim that goodness, we appreciate it far more. As a result, claiming my identity as a child of God has a much deeper meaning for me now.

God's work in me continued on a daily basis. I acquired knowledge and understanding as I reflected on the readings of each day. I learned even more as I reflected on the readings over time. I began to develop a great appreciation for the gift of time. Each liturgical season took on special significance. The accumulation of those seasons into a annual growth cycle became a source of wonder and awe. Each day was unique because of the grace it could bring, and it was part of an annual cycle that served to build my faith as I was privileged to participate in the mysteries of the life of Christ – His incarnation; His public ministry; His passion, death, and resurrection. God had touched my soul deeply through the life of His Son. He was calling me to a life of holiness and showing me *the Way* to achieve it.

My relationship with God had changed my life. My heart was becoming attuned to the heart of God. I was learning to put on the mind of Christ. God's grace had opened my heart to feelings of compassion. It had made my mind like a sponge, eager to learn about the faith which sustained me. I studied the Bible. I read about the lives of saints and allowed their writings to re-pattern my thinking. I spent countless hours studying the audio and video tapes made by theologian Scott Hahn. I wanted to gain an intellectual understanding of the faith that God was allowing me to experience.

I felt inadequate about my knowledge of Scripture. I wanted to more fully understand God's word. In an effort to do that, I bought a hand-held computerized Bible that allowed me to search sacred Scripture for special themes, and quickly identify important quotes that I wanted to review. When I purchased the computer, I put a set of brand new batteries in it. That was over 15 years ago. To this day those same batteries continue to operate that computer. I once shared this story with a priest who responded, "Some computers say *Intel inside*. Yours should say *God inside!*"

Humor is also an important means to growing in holiness. I have found that God has a great sense of humor. When I would get irritated or distressed, He would find ways to lighten my outlook. At times healing can be an exhausting vocation. Occasionally, I would be overcome with a desire to disconnect my phone. One day as I sat with Jesus in the Blessed Sacrament, I was feeling exhausted and overwhelmed. That desire to disconnect my phone was in my heart. As I sat in quiet meditation, a vision came to me of Jesus sitting up in heaven surrounded by telephones that were ringing off the hook. There He sat, in the midst of it all, with a smile on His face and peace in His heart. It was His humorous way of telling me: "Knock off the self-pity, and get back to work. My grace is sufficient for you."

That is probably the most important lesson I learned as I grew in holiness. When I began to trust in Jesus, I learned that His grace *is* sufficient for me. That was the lesson I needed to open the door to the memories from my childhood that were in need of healing.

3

Body of Christ, Save Me.

So much of my life needed to be healed. If I had been able to see clearly and understand the magnitude of my wounds in the beginning of my journey, I would have collapsed in despair. Now I am able to reflect honestly on my former condition because I can see myself through God's eyes – eyes that are filled with wisdom, love, and mercy. God reached out to me through the hand of His Son and taught me the wisdom of the cross. In spite of the countless ways in which I was offending Him, God continued to love me and lead me toward wholeness – holiness.

Through my relationship with Jesus I was able to peel back the layers of sin and decay that prevented the light of Christ from shining through me into the world. Through a friend, God placed into my hands a wonderful little book entitled, "Key to Heaven." It became the *key* to my transformation. God inspired me to use many of the prayers contained in this invaluable book. The prayers that I recall with great fondness are the Devotions to the Sacred Heart. I would sit in front of the tabernacle daily and recite: an Act of Reparation to the Sacred Heart of Jesus, an Act of Consecration to the Most Sacred Heart of Jesus, a litany to the Sacred Heart, and a series of short invocations.*

Note: Readers who are unfamiliar with the Devotions to the Sacred Heart of Jesus are encouraged to read pages 185 to 192 in the Appendix to initiate an understanding of these devotions. Readers who are familiar with Devotions to the Sacred Heart are invited to refresh their memories by participating in these devotions frequently.

These prayers were far more than mere words on a page. They introduced me to the Sacred Heart of Jesus. As I developed an understanding of the Sacred Heart, I could feel my own heart begin to change. One of the short invocations read:

> *Jesus, meek and humble of heart,*
> *Make our hearts like unto Thine.*

Whatever we ask in His Name, we receive. I asked in earnest for my heart to be like His, and the metamorphosis began. One by one He guided me through the items of the litany in an effort to make Himself the true King and Center of my heart. Through the litany He strengthened and remodeled my heart in the image of His own heart. Through the Act of Reparation He showed me the hardness of my heart and how it caused pain and suffering for Him. This inspired a desire for me to let go of my sinful ways and become more like Him. Through the Act of Consecration He taught me to dedicate myself to His Sacred Heart and experience a sense of belonging and unity.

Devotion to the Sacred Heart guided my healing process. It revealed the bitterness I harbored in my heart. Bitterness and lack of forgiveness were toxic emotions that contaminated many relationships in my family. I was subjected to the bitterness of others, and I was a victim of the bitterness that I felt toward them. They sinned, and I sinned in response to their sin; thereby, fueling the perpetual cycle of sin.

In addition to bitterness and lack of forgiveness, somewhere deep inside my heart lurked the hatred and fury that comprised the weak human response to the violence and abuse inflicted on me. By and large the abuse and my reaction to it remained buried in my unconscious mind, but it appeared randomly in my behavior – sometimes in the form of uncontrollable sobbing and tears, other times in outbursts of rage. Self-righteousness was another demon that lived in my heart. It was a family trait that I had adopted, and it interfered in my walk with God. Each of these weaknesses was healed by a softening of my heart, and a corresponding ability to see the world differently.

Self-reliance and independence were obstacles that littered the path separating me from God. They were deeply ingrained in my identity, and somewhat more challenging to heal. In the world these characteristics are held in high esteem; however, they prevented me from entering the path toward true wisdom. The wisdom literature of the Bible states that: "Fear of the Lord is the beginning of wisdom" (Ps. 111:10). I grew to understand that authentic fear of the Lord is a reverential fear that caused me to refrain from offending God because of my love for Him. That same type of fear called me to depend on Him in a way that I have never been able to depend on people.

As the oldest of four children, I was expected to be independent and self-reliant. It was my job to take care of my siblings, help with the housework, and spend long hours helping Dad at the store. There was no time for me to be dependent on anyone for anything. However, little by little God tried to encourage me to be dependent on Him. He made some serious inroads into the process, but I resisted true conversion.

Then God decided to employ drastic measures during one of my trips to Peru. I had been traveling to Peru every few months to offer healing to the people of villa el Salvador – village of the Savior. I had grown quite fond of treating the Peruvian people. Their simple way of life and their deep faith were a source of inspiration and healing for me.

They readily accepted the truth about themselves, and were eager to find healing. As a people they are quite different from the people of the United States, who hide behind layers of false selves and try to dodge the truth about themselves and their situations. Working with the people of villa el Salvador was a refreshing change for me. Their openness took me into a deeper level of my own healing.

Often on my trips to Peru I had several companions. During this special visit, only one other person joined me. Throughout my visit I experienced a number of minor panic attacks. Briefly, I was stricken with fear, but I was always able to move through it and continue my activities. Panic attacks were new to me. I had never experienced them before that time, and I have not experienced them since. I believe they were a gift to me from God – a gift through which He taught me to truly depend on Him.

The panic attacks became more frequent and more intense as we approached the date of my companion's departure. My companion was a priest who was sent by the pastor of my parish to form ties with some of the priests from our sister parish in villa el Salvador. He was the only person who knew about my panic attacks because he was with me when I experienced an attack on a small vehicle the Peruvians use for public transportation. He witnessed my intense fear, and became concerned about the difficulty I had breathing. He was especially apprehensive about leaving me alone in villa el Salvador with no one to accompany me on the journey home. I was also concerned, and yet, determined to proceed with my plans.

Things went well until the day of my departure. The Sisters of the Holy Faith drove me to the airport where I went through the normal departure routine. After several teary "good-byes," I went to the gate to wait for the boarding call. As soon as I arrived at the boarding area, the panic set in. I did everything I could do to distract myself and move through the fear. It was to no avail. The panic continued to mount. I was afraid of being alone. I was afraid of the language barrier. I was afraid of my physical symptoms. I was afraid of being confined to a small space. I was afraid of flying. I was afraid the plane might experience mechanical failure. I was afraid of my fear! My rational mind could not control my fear. It escalated, causing my heart to pound and race inside my chest. My breathing was rapid and shallow. My thoughts were confused. I could talk to no one to calm me in my distress. My only consoling thought was that the plane was scheduled to depart in less than half an hour. I kept telling myself that I would be fine once I boarded the plane. It was an illusion that lasted for a short time.

Shortly after I arrived at the boarding area the flight information board showed my departure as being delayed for two hours. There I was alone and face-to-face with my fear – a fear over which I had no control. Even talking to God did not help. He allowed me to remain in that state of extreme distress until I got on the plane. It seemed like the longest two hours of my life. Apparently, that is how long it took to wear down my attitude of self-reliance and independence. God's message to me was very clear, when I was prepared to hear it: "You cannot save yourself – you need Me."

Self-reliance had allowed me to live in the illusion that I did not need anyone. I was confident and capable of caring for myself. Being dependent on others was totally foreign to me. Consequently, I was unable to genuinely depend on God. This attitude of mine was interfering with my relationship with God, and it had to go. God gave me this opportunity to let go of my self-righteous independence, and He stayed with me until that hardness in my heart crumbled and I achieved the insight He intended.

My struggle with self-reliance did not end on that plane trip home from Peru. On the contrary, it had finally begun in earnest. I made a commitment to God in that moment of crisis. I promised to actively pursue healthy dependence on Him. Every day for months I kneeled in front of the tabernacle and stated my *inability* to depend on Him. Every day I implored His assistance to help me. The honesty of the poor people of Peru inspired me to be honest with myself in my relationship with God. It changed my life by changing my heart.

After that experience, the words "Body of Christ, save me" acquired new meaning. I realized that I could do nothing without Him. Because of this transformation in my thinking, He was able to teach me to *walk in grace*.* I learned to pray before undertaking any activity.* I learned to ask for guidance and assistance in all things, no matter how small or insignificant they seemed. I learned to wait until God's timing moved me forward. I learned to remain steadfast and perseverant in the most difficult circumstances. I changed as a person in all aspects of my identity and in every role that I played in relationship to others. I especially changed as a healer.

Note: *See the Appendix for a meditation to facilitate* **Walking in Grace**. *Also included in the Appendix is a 10 Step Process for Accomplishing Goals through the guidance obtained in prayer and reflection.*

The saving power of God had the power to soften my heart and to transform my mind. It expanded my thinking to help me move beyond a focus on the passing things of this world, and learn to fix my eyes on a world that will never end. This eternal perspective changed the context in which I considered events, relationships, and circumstances. This was the final piece that God put in place to enable me to enter the process that would heal my deepest wounds and help me facilitate healing for others.

From the moment I began to ask for the grace to be dependent on God, He began to reveal to me countless opportunities to find the great wisdom that is stored in the human body. It is truly the Body of Christ that saves us all. His perfect Body is available as a Source of healing for all people. His presence is among us always, resonating with the perfection of true God and true Man. Through Him we can identify our weaknesses, our lack of well-being, our areas of darkness and pain. In Him we can find strength, well-being, light, and healing. With Him we can grow in holiness and deeper union with our Father in heaven. All we need to do is ask, seek, and knock.

4

Blood of Christ, Inebriate Me.

Blood – the miraculous body fluid that gives and sustains life, and promotes healing. Without adequate circulation body tissues will die. Significant blood loss can result in death for an individual.

During life the blood performs three primary functions for the body: transport, protection, and regulation. In its **transport** function, blood *supports* body tissues by delivering oxygen from the lungs, and nutrients from the digestive system, to all parts of the body. It also *detoxifies* the tissues by removing carbon dioxide and metabolic wastes. The transport function of blood aids the *communication* system of the body by carrying hormones from the endocrine glands to their target cells. Because of its ability to carry metabolic heat, the blood helps to *stabilize* body temperature.

The blood is essential for **protection** as well. Blood plays important roles in *managing inflammation* and *healing wounds*. White blood cells (leukocytes) can *destroy invading organisms* and cancerous cells. Platelets (a component of blood) *initiate clotting* and *minimize blood loss*. Blood also helps in body **regulation**. Blood *transfers water* to and from the tissues, keeping them properly hydrated. It *stabilizes water* content in cells, preventing them from shrinking or swelling. In addition, blood helps to *stabilize body pH*, maintaining a health-promoting environment for the cells and allowing enzymes to function normally.

Human blood is vital to the *physical* well-being of the person. The Precious Blood* of Jesus is vital to the *total* well-being of the person. It reaches beyond the physical aspect, touching the mind, the emotions, the spirit, and the soul. Just as the cells of the body cannot survive without human blood, the body/mind/spirit as a whole cannot sustain life without the Precious Blood of Jesus. It purifies the mind. It soothes and stabilizes the emotions. It invigorates the spirit, providing wisdom from above. It heals the wounds of the soul, facilitating clotting to minimize blood loss and restoring a healthy environment to promote healing. The Precious Blood provides the breath of life and the spiritual food needed to sustain us. It warms and protects us. It removes toxic thoughts and feelings that contaminate our self-image and our relationships. It brings vital communication from God to motivate and inspire our thoughts and our actions. The Precious Blood regulates and stabilizes the interdependent functioning among body, mind, emotions, spirit, and soul. It animates us, keeping us alive and well. It circulates through all aspects of the human person, identifying areas of need and facilitating healing.

That is how I have come to view the role of the Precious Blood in my life. It was the Precious Blood that brought me a conscious understanding of the wounds sustained by my mind, my emotions, my spirit, and my soul. These wounds were beyond my conscious awareness, and they were the source of the unbearable physical pain that riddled my entire body. By the time I gave birth to my daughter at the age of 32, I could not recall living without severe,

Note: See the Appendix for Devotions to the Precious Blood.

chronic pain. The pain was my constant companion. It failed to subside, regardless of the treatments that were attempted. In part, it could be traced to two blows to the head during my childhood, and one serious toboggan accident that occurred in my early twenties. Over time I realized that these *accidents* resulted from the efforts of my soul to cry out for help and offer a new direction in my life.

The severe physical pain coupled with the torment of my soul and the upheaval in my emotions created an intolerable living situation in my body. There was no safe or comfortable place for me to reside *down there*. Consequently, my consciousness escaped out the top of my head and controlled the animations of my body in a way that is similar to how a puppeteer guides a marionette. This disconnected and distant relationship between my consciousness and my body was the only way of life I knew, until I became pregnant with my daughter, Lauren. The awesome reality of having a new life growing inside me gave me the courage to re-enter my body.

This new dimension of the Precious Blood as it sustains new life and facilitates the growth of an unborn child became a powerful source of healing for me. My pain was dramatically reduced throughout my pregnancy, partially due to the influence of the Precious Blood and partially due to the release of endorphins. In spite of the constant nausea, I had an improved sense of well-being. I was filled with additional grace that lifted the heaviness of the burden I had grown accustomed to carrying. The infusion of hope, love, and joyful anticipation enabled me to keep my consciousness in my body.

Lauren was delivered by Cesarean section in November. In March of the following year my grandfather died.

These two members of my family lived together on this earth for only a short time. During that time I experienced great anxiety when my grandfather was near Lauren, most especially when he wanted to hold her.

Conscious memories of this man were incongruent with my anxious feelings. He was a good and kind man in my conscious memory. He was funny, and he loved to play with us when we were children. What would cause me to have such anxious feelings toward him when he approached Lauren?

November through March proved to be a difficult time. Lauren was a "colicky" baby who suffered from repeated ear infections. We spent so much time in the pediatrician's office that they offered us an apartment in the basement. At the same time my grandfather became seriously ill and was hospitalized. Before that time I never remembered seeing him sick a day in his life.

Stress was a constant theme for my life in those days. Sleep was a luxury that occurred for short periods of time or on rare occasions. I felt abandoned and isolated. There was no one who came to my aid. Night after night I rocked Lauren in the "brown chair," while she wailed and screamed in agonizing pain. In the morning I would ask my husband why he failed to help us during the night. He claimed that he never heard her screaming. How could that be when there was a baby monitor in both rooms? He never had any answers. Nor did he show any compassion for Lauren's pain or my growing exhaustion.

All of these events proved to be external triggers that served to awaken sleeping memories of a time that was too painful to recall otherwise. During those early months of Lauren's life, my memories were vague and diffuse. The

pain and isolation that I shared nightly with Lauren reso-
nated with the pain and isolation of my early years of abuse.
These remained confusing *feeling memories* until several
years later, when I was taking classes in Process
Acupressure. With no prompting from anyone in my environment, I began to recall the events of my abuse as I lay
on the table receiving work from another student. We were
attending a beginning level workshop that focused merely
on learning to initiate process work. Apparently, the work
that I needed to process was so close to the surface that it
appeared as soon as we began.

During this "practice session" I experienced a segment
of the abuse from my grandfather and clearly saw his face.
It was the beginning of a long and arduous process that
continued until Lauren was nine years old. In Lauren's
ninth year, things began to change. Even though seasonal
memories continued to occur according to the satanic cal-
endar, the experience of those memories was different.
Somehow, I knew that the abuse had ended when I was
nine. Years later, when I had the courage to look at family
photo albums, I realized that I was unable to identify myself as the "girl in the picture" at my mother's family gath-
erings during my early years. An entire piece of my life
had been encapsulated and set apart from my conscious
memory.

I received no support from my family during this painful process of recollection. Even though my mother (who
was several hours away from the location of the workshop)
was traumatized during the precise hours of my first
memory recall at the Process Acupressure workshop, she
refused to accept the truth of my experience then, and she
continues to refuse the truth now. She could not think of
her father as the man I described. After years of invasive

memories and repeated affirmations of past events, it is still difficult for me to believe as well. However, the evidence remains. My mother and I have suffered from endless and varied symptoms of illness and chronic pain throughout our lives. As I found the courage to see and know the truth, my healing began. My intense, chronic pain is now gone. I have a wonderful sense of well-being, and my relationships with God and others are strong and vital. By His wounds I have been healed.

However, the actual recovery process was long and arduous. The invasive memories appeared spontaneously and randomly. Present events served as triggers for past trauma. Some were sudden one time events, like the experience I had at Knoeble's amusement park. Lauren loved train rides as a child. We had ridden them often together. However, most of them were indoors or in a fantasy-type environment. The train ride at Knoeble's was very different. It was a much larger train, and it traveled outside the amusement area of the park and into a nearby wooded area. Lauren and I were talking and laughing as we rode. I turned to look ahead as we approached a u-turn on the tracks. Suddenly, I was transported into the past, recalling an episode of the abuse that had taken place in a wooded area near the railroad tracks. Many times these invasive memories occurred to provide an opportunity to move through the trauma and release the trapped memories. I believe that this particular recollection entered my conscious mind in order to stop the doubts I had been having about the reality of the abuse. There was no way I could have consciously created such an experience.

In addition to one-time events, there were seasonal memories and certain daily events that created a nagging sense of discomfort. The best example of this is my anxiety about allowing Lauren to take the bus to school. There was no anxiety about her going to school or visiting friends; however, I never felt comfortable letting her ride the bus, even when she was in high school. One day I was talking to her about being careful riding the bus and she replied, "Mom, how old do I have to be before you can trust me to ride the bus. You've been telling me the same thing since I was in kindergarten." That day I realized that my anxiety about Lauren riding the bus was tied to my past. My grandfather drove a school bus. Even though no unconscious memories of the abuse were tied to the school bus, there remained some connection between my conscious and unconscious mind regarding school buses.

Flashbacks, invasive memories, and anxiety are several ways that the unconscious mind communicates with the conscious mind to provide opportunities for healing wounds created by past traumatic events. Body memories provide a very different means of healing wounds. Body memories can emerge during a bodywork session, as described in the recounting of my first Process Acupressure session. Body memories can also occur spontaneously, creating tremendous confusion and intense pain. The deluge of body memories that was associated with my healing process was overwhelming, especially during the early years of discovery. Much of my physical pain was connected to the wounds that were inflicted on my mind, my emotions, and my soul as a result of the abuse. It seemed as though God took advantage of every possible opportunity to bring forth healing for me.

One of the most intense periods of healing took place in Fatima, Portugal, while I was on pilgrimage. The young visionaries who experienced the apparitions in Fatima were given a glimpse of hell. My visit to Fatima, although wonderful in many ways, was a personal experience of hell. Filled with flashbacks and body memories, God used every minute of my trip toward the purpose of making me whole.

I had a lovely older woman for a roommate. We got along very well. I spent a good deal of time helping her get from place to place because she suffered from pain in her knees. She felt terribly indebted to me as a result of my kindness to her. It presented no hardship for me at all. I was delighted to help her. Even though we spent nearly all of our time together, she had no knowledge of the suffering that I was enduring until one day when the body memories caused pain beyond what I could bear. I laid in bed suffering quietly for hours.

The pain was in my head and my face. Because of the years I had spent struggling with severe pain, I was able to tolerate extraordinary levels of pain and remain functional. Throughout my life very few people knew that I was suffering. The pain I experienced in Fatima was different. I could not conceal it. My breathing was rapid and shallow. Tears poured down my face for hours. I tried working on myself to no avail. There seemed to be no relief in sight. Concerned for my well-being, my roommate asked if I would allow her to pray over me. I invited her to help in any way she could. She prayed aloud for sometime, holding her hands over me. I recall only that she asked for the Precious Blood of Jesus to wash over me and heal my pain.

My anxiety and stress eased immediately, bringing a corresponding reduction in the pain. My mind continued to focus on the concept of being washed by the Precious Blood. I felt as though the Precious Blood was able to penetrate deep within my wounds and bring comfort and healing. I rested for several hours surrounded by the Precious Blood, realizing that it was a familiar experience even though it had never been part of my conscious understanding. The Precious Blood had been with me throughout my times of suffering. It had given me the strength to endure and persevere. It had provided the courage for me to enter into the memories of my abuse. It had initiated the healing process for each of my wounds and given me the fortitude to see the process through to completion. It was the Precious Blood that was responsible for all aspects of my healing. Even though the healing was facilitated through some form of bodywork or counseling or movement therapy, the underlying Source of all my healing was the Precious Blood of Jesus. The Blood that poured from His wounds as He hung on the cross mystically infused my wounds, creating an opportunity for me to heal – physically, mentally, emotionally, and spiritually.

The Precious Blood brought nourishment and support to the wounded tissue of my body. It released the toxic effects of the trauma from all levels of my being. It brought clotting to the massive wounds in my soul that had continued to bleed. In a nonverbal way, it communicated God's love for me and His desire to make me whole. It surrounded my wounds with a protective mantle, giving them time to heal more fully. The Precious Blood stabilized the areas impacted by trauma, and facilitated normalization and regulation.

As long as my vision was restricted to the here and now, I attributed the healing I received to the things of this world – things that I could see and name. When God granted me the grace to see from an eternal perspective, it became clear to me that the ultimate Source of all healing is the Precious Blood of Jesus Christ. Through the Precious Blood

I was inebriated with love – a love that has the power to heal.

The healing process has occurred to such an extent that it is now comfortable for me to dwell in any part of my body. My consciousness can flow freely into all parts of my mind. It can explore my emotions, and take direction to act based on how I feel and the appropriateness of the behavior. My will is strong and attuned to the will of God. My spirit feels alive and well, and my soul has been healed and made whole.

Through the power of the Precious Blood, Jesus has entered the parts of me that were filled with darkness and woe. He has healed my wounds, providing light and a sense of well-being. By His wounds I have been healed.

5

Water Flowing from the Side of Christ, Wash Me.

In the account of the crucifixion as it is recorded by John, the gospel states that "when they came to Jesus and saw that He was already dead, they did not break His legs, but one soldier thrust his lance into His side, and immediately blood and water flowed out" (Jn. 19:33-34). Through faith we have the ability to enter into living Scripture and stand at the foot of the cross. When we stand at the foot of the cross, we have the opportunity to be bathed in the water that flowed from the side of Christ and be washed with the life-giving water that Jesus offered to the woman at the well. Jesus told the woman at the well "the water I shall give will become ... a spring of water welling up to eternal life" (Jn. 4-14). This life-giving water can be consumed or we can be immersed in it. The important thing is our contact with the water as a symbol of our faith.

The mysteries of our faith can present intellectual challenges for us at times. This is especially true with the mystery of the Precious Blood and the mystery of the water. Water and blood are both concrete substances to which we can relate on a natural level. They can be seen and touched, making them very real for us. However, when we are called to enter into the mysteries of our faith, both water and blood take on a mystical reality that requires abstract thinking and use of the intuitive mind. Consequently, entering into the mysteries of our faith requires a shift in thinking. The concrete processing rational mind must become quiet, and allow the intuitive mind to expand and interact with the abstract aspect of the rational mind. Through this mental shift we let go of our desire to control, and open our ability to explore, using the gift of childlike curiosity – a gift that is fueled by wonder and awe. We can only appreciate the mysteries of our faith by freely exploring living Scripture with the combined gifts of abstract reasoning and intuitive thinking. From this perspective we can enter into the mystery and experience it as it unfolds. This is how we learn the wisdom of God through reflection and meditation.

Many individuals find this process to be quite difficult. Consequently, they fail to receive the abundant benefits that are available to those who can and do meditate on the mysteries of God regularly. I believe that our God is a God who provides choices. Surely He would not want the wonderful benefits of meditation to be wasted or totally inaccessible. I have found that the gift of faith that is symbolized by water can be revealed and solidified through meditation. It can also be acknowledged and anchored in the body through acupressure. The same is true of the blood.

Acupressure is based on the ancient Chinese healing art, acupuncture. The Chinese believe that there are Five Elements in the body. They are all part of one interconnected system that includes the major organs and a system of energetic pathways that flow throughout the body. Fire and Water are two of the five elements. Blood belongs to the Fire Element. To facilitate better understanding, only the Water Element will be considered in detail. However, a similar analysis can be used for the Fire Element and its influence on the blood.

Each of the Five Elements exists on a continuum that goes through a range that includes excess, balance, and deficiency. When we are strong in our faith, a healthy Water Element makes us bold and courageous. We can face great obstacles and challenges based on the strength that dwells within us. This is the strength that Jesus demonstrated during His passion. Similar strength could be found in the Christian martyrs – those who died for the faith. There are also individuals who are very strong in their faith, but have not been called to demonstrate that strength by surrendering their lives. These individuals all have a balanced Water Element.

If we imagine the Water Element as it would be diagrammed on a horizontal line, balanced Water would appear in the center of the line. The remaining two characteristics of Water would be found on opposite ends of the line (see diagram below). A deficiency in Water would be manifested in a person who was fearful; while an excess in Water would be manifested in a person with foolhardy behavior. In the Chinese model the goal is to become centered and balanced. For the Water Element this means being bold and courageous. Those who are balanced in Water have the gift of fortitude, as well as the grace to appreciate life with an attitude of wonder and awe.

(-) (Deficiency)	**BALANCE**	(+) (Excess)
Fearful	**Courageous**	*Foolhardy*

The objective of receiving acupressure treatments is to help the individual achieve and maintain balance. A fearful person can begin to overcome fear by receiving acupressure treatments to balance the Water Element, and individuals who have experienced fearful life events can be released from that fear by balancing the Water Element. For example, a woman came to me recently complaining that she felt as though she had a ball stuck in her throat. As I worked to return the tissue of the throat to balance, I sensed trauma residing in the tissue. When I asked if she had experienced a life-threatening incident that involved the tissue in her throat, she said that she had recently choked on a pill and was afraid that she would not be able to breathe again. She actually thought that she was going to die. In addition to the trauma in her throat, the entire back of her body was stiff. The bladder meridian, part of the Water Element, travels down the back of the head, torso, and legs. Fear from the choking incident was anchored in her bladder meridian, causing her entire back to become stiff. Releasing the trauma from her throat and balancing the bladder meridian brought her entire body back into balance as it released the fear she was holding. This is only one example of the type of healing that can be facilitated through acupressure.

The diagram of the Water Element as seen on page 43 can be viewed from an entirely secular perspective, as evidenced in the example described above. It can also be used in a Christian context by allowing the center point for **courage** to be infused with the gifts of fortitude and piety, two of the seven gifts of the Holy Spirit.

Many people see the model of the Five Elements and assume that the energetic pathways are some form of *universal energy*. They call this energy *chi*. I believe that this energy is, in fact, the Holy Spirit* that Jesus discussed during His discourse at the Last Supper. When the meridians of the body are balanced by and for people of faith, that faith is enlivened and fortified. We are able to move beyond the worldly benefits of bodywork and enter into the mysteries of our faith. Consequently, repeated balancing of the Water Element helps individuals more fully embrace and live the truths of their faith.

Just as meditation allows us to enter into the mysteries of our faith, acupressure opens similar doors to the supernatural realm. Through meditation we can have a personal encounter with Jesus. That communion transfigures us more in His image. Acupressure performed in a Christian context provides an encounter by two individuals who are gathered in His name. Trained hands can access the Holy Spirit within the person who is being treated, and bring forth healing that is ordained by the will of God. That healing is accomplished through the sacred Body of Christ whose perfect image resonates with wholeness, touching the lowly body being treated, and bringing light and well-being into areas that were filled with darkness and woe.

Having spent countless hours in both meditation and healing work, I can attest to the similarity of the experiences. Prayer and meditation in front of the Blessed Sacrament infuses me with the gift of faith, among many other gifts. Balancing the Water Element, while honoring the presence of Christ between two people working together toward healing, also infuses both of them with the gift of faith. Life-giving water flowing from the side of Christ

Note: See the Appendix for Devotions to the Holy Spirit.

has an opportunity to touch us while we are in direct communion with Him, and when we find communion with Him through our interactions with others. This deepening of faith that occurs through simple faith sharing can be anchored in the body with bodywork.

Often people comment about the strength of my faith. I believe that my strong faith has evolved through meditation, healing of myself, and healing of others. I spend a lot of time standing at the foot of the cross being washed by the water flowing from the side of Jesus. I also drink the living water that Jesus offered to the woman at the well. Both strengthen my faith, creating within me "a spring of water welling up to eternal life." The strength of my faith enabled me to participate in the healing process God chose for me. Participating in the healing process, in turn, further strengthened my faith. God led me by the hand and helped me enter a healing spiral that initiated a constant evolution in my faith.

6

Passion of Christ, Strengthen Me.

Of all the mysteries of the life of Christ, I feel closest to the passion. Since my life was one of suffering, I was comfortable meeting Jesus during His moments of suffering. He taught me to walk the way of the cross early in our journey together. Even though I had experienced tremendous suffering, I actually knew very little about it until Jesus called me to walk with Him to Calvary every Friday, and occasionally on other days during the week.

Until I came to know Jesus, suffering and pain were sources of bitterness in my heart. They were things that I *had to endure,* or things that I *tried very hard to escape or ignore.* Instead of accepting pain and suffering, I attempted to tolerate it. Acceptance leads to healing, while tolerance results in stagnation and exhaustion. By accepting the pain and owning it as a part of my life, I learned to move through the pain and find healing. It is very common for those who suffer to dissociate from the pain. After all pain is pain, and suffering is suffering. Who wants to have any part in that? It is human nature to seek pleasure and avoid pain. Through the wisdom of the cross I learned to transcend that aspect of my human nature, and surrender to the reality of the human condition – a life that includes pain and suffering. I actually began to experience *joy* in my suffering because I realized that pain and suffering brought with them invaluable lessons and a closeness to

Jesus that made it all worthwhile. I am grateful for my life just as it was. My experiences have made me who I am today – the person God created me to be. I take great delight in the grace I have to facilitate healing in the lives of others. Through suffering and pain, I learned to embrace the cross, and I developed the gift to heal.

Jesus asked the sons of Zebedee: "Can you drink the cup that I am going to drink?" They replied, "We can." (Mt. 20-22) I wonder if they really understood what He was asking them. Liquid that is consumed from the cup of suffering can be very hard to swallow. Jesus gives testimony to that later in Matthew's gospel during the agony in the garden. While Peter and the sons of Zebedee are sleeping, Jesus falls prostrate in prayer, saying: "My Father, if it is possible, let this cup pass from me; yet, not as I will, but as you will" (Mt. 26:39). Jesus accepted the cup of suffering and did the will of the Father. The sons of Zebedee failed to simply remain with Him and keep watch as He experienced the agony in the garden. How easy it is to give lip service – how difficult it is to fulfill the commitment.

I spent years of my life asking for the *cup to pass from me* by rejecting the pain and suffering in my life. When I responded to the call to remain with Him and keep watch, my entire life changed. Instead of sleeping through – ignoring – my pain and suffering, I learned to embrace it as Jesus embraced His cross. I walked side-by-side with Him, listening to the story of His passion and allowing it to transform my weak human heart more in the image of His Sacred Heart.

Acceptance was my lesson. It was only possible after I had learned to depend on God. Faith taught me to trust in Him, knowing that goodness would result in the end. The wisdom of the cross taught me that there is always a resurrection after the crucifixion. Before I learned to walk with Jesus, I had tried to carry my crosses on my own, failing to depend on God. I seemed to have superhuman endurance. I would pick up the cross and drag it from place to place. When it became more than I could bear, I experienced a type of crucifixion. Basically, I would simply collapse from exhaustion. After lying in a heap of spent humanity, I would get up and take up the same cross, or perhaps a different one to add a little variety to the experience. Once again, I would drag it from place to place, only to collapse in exhaustion. Never was I taken down from the cross by others who loved me. Never was I tended with spices and perfumed oils. Never was I tenderly laid in the tomb to rest with Jesus and be prepared for the resurrection.

I was trapped in a vicious cycle of needless suffering. The love of Christ – in His passion, death, and resurrection – changed all of that for me. Over and over and over again, He allowed me to experience the passion with Him. He allowed me to look into the eyes of the mother who loved Him, and gain strength from the loving relationship that they shared. He allowed me to rest in the arms of our Father in heaven throughout His experience of the passion to help me grow in my understanding of the way of the cross.* He pulled me beneath His Sacred Body as we fell, protecting me from the beating inflicted by the soldiers. He taught me to allow others, like Simon and Veronica, to come to my aid in times of need. He taught me to allow the things of this world to be stripped from me like His

---

Note: See the Appendix for a set of Stations of the Cross entitled: By His Wounds You are Healed.

garments were stripped from Him. He taught me to focus on eternal things – things that no one could take from Him or from me. He hid me in His wounds and covered me with His Precious Blood, allowing me to heal and be made whole. All of these profound lessons were mine because I walked the way of the cross with Jesus. However, the most important thing I learned was that there is an end to carrying the cross. I can be taken down from the cross, tended, and laid to rest beside Him. Together, we can be prepared for and participate in the resurrection.

In the agony in the garden, Jesus experienced the pain and brokenness of humanity, both personally and collectively. Through His humility and obedience to God, Jesus brought the power and majesty of God into the deepest wounds of our human condition. From the agony in the garden, He walked the way of the cross, carrying our wounds in His flesh. Symbolically, these wounds were manifested in His physical body as He was scourged, crowned with thorns, crucified, and pierced.

His wounds went beyond mere physical tissue. He also experienced the pain of abandonment and rejection, as well as the shame of the cross. He experienced the human sense of desperation that accompanies such intensely painful moments, and He cried out *for us*: "My God, my God, why have you abandoned me?" (Ps. 22:2) Our God knows personally what it is like to be wounded physically, mentally, emotionally and spiritually. He tasted the pain we have experienced in difficult relationships that involve intense suffering. Regardless of how we have suffered, Jesus understands because He chose to suffer with us and for us.

Knowing that suffering is a very real part of our human experience. Jesus willingly suffered *as God*, but he did it from a human perspective. He remains with us always, keeping true to His word: "I will not leave you orphans, I will come to you." (Jn. 14:15) Even when we cannot or will not come to Him, He comes to us. Our lives are in His hands; loving, caring, compassionate hands that hold us, caress us, and go before us to prepare a place for us. (Jn. 14:2)

The passion of Christ was given to us to provide healing and growth. The reality of the passion exists perpetually throughout time, giving us constant access to opportunities for growth and healing. Because God is constant and the mystery of the cross is perpetually available, our human disposition is the only variable aspect in our process of healing and growth. Our perspective, our responses, and our capacity to relate to the mystery of God determine the process of our healing and growth.

In our humanity we can either be open-minded or closed-minded. We can choose to see the mystery of the cross as a perpetual sacrifice that offers an open door to heaven and a life in relationship with God. Or we can deny the cross because of shame, ignorance, fear, selfishness, pride or some other human weakness. By closing our minds to the love and the saving power of God, we "put God in a box" and we place limitations on our own growth and healing. Sometimes we limit ourselves to the point of suffocation and death. Isn't it ironic that suffocation was the cause of death for the One who came to give us life?

We can also limit the power and goodness of God by seeing the crucifixion and death of our Lord as merely an historical event. If we convince ourselves that it happened somewhere back in time, that it is an event in the distant past, far away from us and our present lives, we discount the very power of God that saves us and sets us free.

The distortions of the human mind can present the crucifixion as an event that is "bigger than life." It can be viewed as something "too big to be real." Once again, this perspective is destructive to our health and well-being. It separates us from the power of God to heal our lives and help us grow in our relationship with Him.

Pause for a moment now and participate in a self-assessment process. How do you see the crucifixion? Is it an open door for you to heal and grow, OR is it closed, giving no access to healing and growth? Is the crucifixion a distant historical event for you, OR is it a perpetual sacrifice that offers healing, consolation and growth? Do you see the crucifixion as being "bigger than life" and too overwhelming to draw close and enter in, OR is it an opportunity for you to stand at the foot of the cross as the Beloved Disciple? Throughout your life, how have you related to the cross of Christ? In what ways could you change this view to make it more pleasing to God and more beneficial to your own healing and growth?

The human mind is one aspect of our being that can either facilitate our relationship with God or create an obstacle in our path. Just as we have the choice to be open-minded or closed-minded, we also have the choice to allow our hearts to be opened by compassion or closed by fear, pride, hatred or selfishness. Our choice determines our ability to heal and grow.

Consider the following questions. Use them as an assessment to determine the condition of your heart. How attuned are you to your own feelings about suffering? What happens to your heart when you think about suffering? Is it open and filled with love just like the arms of Christ are stretched out and open to you from the cross?

Does compassion flow from your heart as the water and blood flowed from His wounded side? Are you able to reflect with wonder and awe concerning His love for you? OR are you afraid of suffering, choosing to avoid it at all costs and filled with disdain at the thought of participating in suffering as a part of life? Are you angry with God because of the existence of suffering? Do you feel that He is unfair and wrong to allow suffering to occur? How do you feel about suffering? Are those feelings helping you to heal and grow? What does God have to say to you about suffering?

A final area to consider is how you relate to people who suffer. Often it is the same way we relate to Jesus as One who has suffered. Sometimes suffering is so painful we wish we could take it away. Sometimes in our efforts to ease suffering and pain we carry the cross for others, instead of allowing them to carry their own cross and participate in their own growth and healing. Other times we smother them with praise or gifts in order to make them feel better or to ease our own guilt. There are also instances when we refuse to look at the suffering and pain of others.

There are those of us, however, who have been given the grace and the courage to walk with those who suffer, even enduring their suffering to a certain extent. Those who have learned the virtue of honoring suffering and the redemptive work that it accomplishes have also learned to remain steadfast and supportive to others in their times of hardship and suffering. Living the mystery of the cross with Jesus helps us to heal both our perspective about and our attitude toward suffering. Living in the mystery of the cross helps us to grow in strength and in virtue, enabling us to walk to Calvary with Him and stand at the foot of the cross. Then when our brothers and sisters in Christ need our help during their trials or hardships, we can come to their aid in an authentic and mature Christian manner, reaching out to them as Jesus reaches out to us through the perpetual vision of the crucifixion.

Regardless of your current perspective and attitude toward suffering, I invite you to join me throughout the next few chapters as I share my personal exploration of the mystery of suffering.

7

O Good Jesus, Hear Me.
Hide Me within Your Wounds.

Suffering is something that I understood rather well as a result of my own experience. When I decided to return to college and get a masters degree in counseling from Franciscan University, I was intrigued by the opportunity to study the mystery of human suffering from an intellectual perspective. While taking a course entitled Human and Spiritual Integration, I read a collection of writings that addressed this subject. I found that an intellectual understanding of suffering can be useful; however, a solely intellectual understanding of suffering seems woefully inadequate as a method for healing the wounds of suffering.

The books I studied were wonderfully written. They offered psychological, philosophical, and theological words of wisdom, comfort, consolation, and even practical advice. Yet they remained painfully inadequate from the perspective of one who has suffered much.

This reality troubled my heart. It was as though my experience of suffering and healing had taken me far beyond the words that have been written to aid humankind in understanding suffering. I struggled with the discrepancy between the needs we have in our moments of suffering, and the tools we have been given to meet those needs. Clearly, there was a missing link. Somehow, I needed to share my own journey with others in an effort to demonstrate the deep and profound healing that can be experienced by walking with God.

I became captivated by the desire to understand the link between human suffering and healing. As my heart and mind struggled to gain a clearer understanding of human suffering, my earnest desire was offered as a prayer to the Father. The struggle for understanding continued for about two months. Never did I proceed with a task-oriented attitude, as if on a mission to conquer the mystery of suffering. Instead, I allowed myself to be immersed in the mystery and participate in the process of unfolding.

During this time God presented reading material to me through my professors at the university. I read the material, and I prayed about it as I offered it up to God for His blessing. I remained simultaneously grateful for the intellectual understanding and frustrated by its lack of power to touch me and heal me in my suffering.

"Something is missing," I kept repeating to God. I knew that the grace of suffering went far beyond the human words I was reading. I wanted to help others enter into the mystery of suffering and find healing for themselves. Our God is a God of the mind and the intellect. More importantly, however, our God is a God of the heart who enters into every life experience with us. This is the God I know. This is the God who touches people through my hands, causing them to proclaim: "If I had known your God, I never would have left the faith."

The struggle ended on November 1, 2002 – the feast of All Saints. Order began to emerge through the chaos, and light began to shine in the darkness. In my prayer I was given an image – not yet in its fullness – but powerful enough to begin the journey that weaves the beauty and goodness of our earthly experiences with the wonder and awe of God's creative mind.

The trigger for this image had occurred during one of my classes the previous week. We had submitted reflection papers on Viktor Frankl's book, "Man's Search for Meaning." Frankl, a survivor of the concentration camps of WWII, asserts that we find meaning in life through work, suffering, and an appreciation of beauty. In our papers we were instructed to reflect on this idea as it related to us individually. I briefly shared the story of my personal suffering – a story that deeply touched the professor. During class, without revealing my situation, she mentioned consoling words that she offers in counseling sessions to those whose suffering is deep and difficult to comprehend. She explained how she tells her clients: "Jesus shed tears from the cross for *your* suffering." In that moment I heard those words as if I were her client, not her student.

I carried those words in my heart for two days. On the feast of All Saints they began to manifest as a *healing image* to help people better understand and accept the reality of human suffering. The image that first appeared was of the crucified Lord. Jesus appeared in the foreground, hanging on a cross. His mother and the Beloved disciple stood at the foot of the cross.

Through my internal vision I gazed at the image from a distance. Many aspects of the crucifixion scene appeared simultaneously – the conversation between Jesus and the two criminals, the words spoken by Jesus to His Mother and John, the blood and water flowing from the wounded side of Jesus, the onset of darkness, the torn veil, the moment of death. It was as if, instead of seeing the crucifixion as a moment in time, or a sequence of events, I saw a perpetual living image that held the entire mystery of the crucifixion as it exists in eternity, giving me, the onlooker, an opportunity to enter into the mystery through any aspect, according to the will of God.

It was as if, in that moment, I received the grace of an experiential awareness of the entire crucifixion scenario. Grace filled me with wonder and awe for some time. Unable to digest the enormity of the experience, it felt as though I was watching a video that was allowed to rest on pause until I could recover from the impact of the vision. It allowed me to move beyond my sense of being overwhelmed, and once again participate in the grace of the mystery.

As I re-entered the mystery, I found myself lying at the feet of Jesus as He hung on the cross above me. With my head at His feet, I looked up to see Him looking down at me from the cross. His compassion for my suffering showed in the tears that fell from His eyes. In that moment I knew that each second of my suffering on this earth was spent at the foot of the cross. Constantly, Jesus was gazing down at me with tears in His eyes, reflecting the compassion in His heart and His burning desire for me to know that I was never alone. The words of Jesus in the gospel of John came to me: "I will not leave you orphans; *I will come to you.*" (Jn. 14:18).

He never said I had to come to Him. He said He would come to me, and He did. In every moment that I had ever suffered throughout my life, Jesus had been with me. When I was an infant and too young to know the story of His life, death and resurrection – Jesus was with me when I suffered. When I was paralyzed by fear and unable to pray – He was with me. If for any reason I could not call His name – He came anyway and He stayed throughout my hour of need.

I realized that through my suffering I, too, became a beloved disciple of the Lord. I had the privilege to rest my head on the Sacred Heart of Jesus. I was called to follow Him and enter into the very mystery of God, finding reassurance in the words Jesus used to explain the feelings of rejection that are often the source of human suffering:

> *If the world hates you, realize that it hated Me first. If you belonged to the world, the world would love its own; but because you do not belong to the world, and I have chosen you out of the world, the world hates you. Remember the word I spoke to you, "No slave is greater than his master." If they persecuted Me, they will also persecute you. If they kept My word, they will also keep yours. And they will do all these things to you on account of My name, because they do not know the One who sent Me (Jn. 15:18-21).*

The words of His promise to those who endure suffering are recorded in the high priestly prayer that Jesus made to the Father just before His passion:

> *And I have given them the glory You gave Me, so that they may be one, as We are one, I in them and You in Me, that they may be brought to perfection as one, that the world may know that You sent Me, and that You loved them even as You loved Me (Jn. 17: 22- 23).*

Rather than hearing these words, I experienced their power to touch and heal. The gates of heaven were opened to me in a way that I had never experienced. I understood that the *privilege of suffering* provides us with the opportunity to make a choice. The two criminals who died on either side of Jesus represent the choice we are able to make in our suffering. Unlike Jesus, they were separated from God by their sins. One criminal chose to express anger, bitterness and resentment, blaming God and demanding to be saved. He was selfishly focused on the moment and his desire to escape pain and death. His vision was limited. It did not include a view of eternity.

The second criminal was about to suffer and die as well, yet he did not harbor the same hardness of heart as the other man. Instead, he recognized that, as criminals, they indeed were suffering greatly, receiving what they deserved for their deeds. Realizing that Jesus had done nothing wrong and that He had the power to save him, the second criminal said, "Jesus, remember me when you come in your Kingdom" (Lk. 23:42).

This second criminal represents our opportunity for acceptance. In our moments of suffering we can accept our woeful human condition with all its faults and failings. We can accept Christ as the Light and Savior of the world. And we can accept the gift of God's love for us as it is demonstrated through the incarnation, the crucifixion, and the promise of the resurrection.

But wait, you might say: some of the suffering that I endured was not my fault. Sometimes I was an innocent victim, suffering for no apparent reason. In these circumstances, we need to redirect our thinking and focus on Christ, the most innocent victim. He embraced the cross, accepting the will of the Father, and seeing this as an opportunity to give glory to God by accomplishing the work He was sent to do. Again, we look to the words of Jesus:

> *I glorified You on earth by accomplishing the*
> *work that You gave Me to do. Now glorify Me,*

*Father, with You, with the glory that I had with
You before the world began. I revealed Your name
to those whom you gave me out of the world.
They belonged to You, and You gave them to Me,
and they have kept Your word (Jn. 17:4-6).*

Hence, whether we are guilty (like the criminals) or innocent (like Christ), acceptance is the choice we are called
to make as Christians. Acceptance allows us to move forward in life. It allows us to grow and develop greater fullness as we share life more intimately with God, uniting
our suffering to the suffering of His Son. This offers us the
privilege to participate in Jesus' redemptive work on earth
– the work that serves to glorify the Father and enables us
to share in His promise.

Having received such extensive insight, you might think
my experience of the crucifixion was complete. Perhaps
you are expecting to hear Jesus say, "It is finished." (Jn.
19:30). Instead, I was privileged to experience two additional passages from the gospel of John.

Once again, I became aware of myself lying at the feet
of Jesus. This time blood and water flowed from His pierced
side. The same love that caused blood and water to flow
from the wounded side of Jesus had surrounded me in every moment of my suffering. His love had penetrated the
deepest, darkest aspects of my trauma. Everything that I
had experienced was being purified and made whole – holy.
The blood and the water became a source of healing and
of strength. Suffering that could have been interpreted as
needless and worthless was being transformed into redemptive suffering. Jesus was saying to me:

> *It was not you who chose Me, but I who chose you and appointed you to go and bear fruit that will remain, so that whatever you ask the Father in My name He may give you (Jn. 15:16).*

As the reality of these words continued to make their way into my consciousness, I became aware of being held in a most tender and gentle way. I found myself mystically lying in the arms of the Mother of Jesus – the mother who was given to the Beloved Disciple at the foot of the cross. She held me in a way that I had longed to be held each time I had suffered. The tenderness of her love has the power to heal and soothe wounds, just as she healed and soothed the wounds of her Son throughout His life and after His death. Resting in her arms, I recalled the words of Jesus:

> *Peace I leave with you; My peace I give to you. Not as the world gives do I give it to you. Do not let your hearts be troubled or afraid (Jn. 14:27).*

As I rested in the arms of the Blessed Mother and the peace of Christ, I felt completely healed and whole, and yet, it was only the beginning of the process.

8

Never Let Me be Separated from You.

In my walk with God I have found that the insight He imparts through meditative experiences is often followed by periods of silence. It is as if He pauses to allow me to digest and assimilate the wisdom He desires me to comprehend. Sometimes these periods of silence are used by God to prepare me to understand and accept the knowledge that is to come.

For several days after the meditative experience described in the previous chapter, I reflected on God's connection to His people. The basis for this reflection was the creation stories told in the book of Genesis. The reflection formed a logical sequence in my thinking, preparing me to receive the next meditation. The following paragraphs summarize my thought sequence.

The first story of creation describes how God brought order from chaos. It describes the emergence of darkness and light. With each stage of the process God sees how good it is. Consequently, the fundamental reality of the created order is good. In particular there is goodness in the men and women who are created in the image of God to participate in a life with God.

In our oneness with God we have the opportunity to experience the delight God has for us. There is a delight that glows and radiates from the heart of God each time a new baby is formed in His likeness and brought first into the world, then ultimately into His kingdom. The joy that we experience as new parents is like the joy that God experienced at the dawn of creation. These are the first feelings shared with us by God. They are the deepest and most authentic feelings we know as human beings.

However, these feelings are sometimes masked, hidden, or buried by our human suffering. Because of the fall, evil and darkness entered the goodness of God's created order. The entrance of evil was not merely an act that occurred at any particular moment in time. Rather, it became a force of darkness that changed the appearance of the created order as it was seen by human beings during this journey in time. However, the goodness of the created order remains in eternity, calling always for us to return to that order. We are out of touch with that order because we are blind and bound in a world of darkness. Yet, the hunger and thirst for this first created order that exists in eternity never leaves us. It may be disguised and hidden. But it remains with us just as Jesus remains with us always.

Our struggles to find light in areas of darkness allow God to reveal to us a hidden desire for goodness, beauty, truth and oneness with Him. He knows that we are blind to the authentic desire that dwells in us. He knows that we are held captive in sin. To help us He sent His Son to heal us and set us free. One of our primary tasks as Christians is to put on the mind of Christ. This enables us to see things in their proper order. It destroys the force of evil that keeps us blind, and it breaks the bonds of sin that hold us bound.

After this "thought sequence" solidified in my mind, I began to experience a series of meditations that were entirely initiated and guided by God. The first meditation began during Mass as we entered into the liturgy of the

Eucharist*. It was like simultaneously *being swept away* **and** *being fully present* in the same moment – a precious moment of insight offered to me as a gift from God.

I was infused by a profound and eternal peace. My eyes closed gently, but firmly, and did not open until God's hand had completed my internal experience. I was filled with a sense of wonder and awe, somehow knowing I was about to enter deeply into a mystery. I received the grace of understanding that would allow me to participate in the mystery. I was filled with the excitement of anticipation, and yet, perfectly patient in allowing the mystery to unfold before me.

At first I was in the role of an observer. It was as if I had a set of binoculars held to my eyes. They had a very wide angle and through them I could see into the distance without end. It was an open, expansive vision. Throughout the meditation I had the capacity to experience a panoramic view and at the same time to zoom in on certain areas.

Through God's grace I came to realize that I was able to see simultaneous realities. It was as if the linear time line of world history filled my view from left to right in the foreground, and beyond the confines of time and space my vision was filled with the essence of eternity.

Note: The Eucharist is a re-enactment of the Last Supper. The prayers and readings in a Eucharistic service are a reminder of the solemn words and actions of our Lord before His death. Eucharist means "thanksgiving." It refers to the sacrament of the Lord's Supper, in which bread and wine became the Body and Blood of Christ.

It was as though time and space were entirely supported and guided by eternity. There were also areas on the timeline that looked like tunnels connecting time and space to eternity. The moments that were clear to me during this particular meditative experience were the creation of the world, the incarnation and the crucifixion. It was clear that there were other times as well, but the events mentioned above were the ones highlighted in my present experience.

Suddenly, I simply understood the process that connects the natural and supernatural events resulting from prayer. When we are compelled to pray by the fervent desire in our hearts, that desire proceeds from us through a mystery in the life of Christ and enters eternity. The power of God then sets things in motion to prepare us and others who are involved in the process or the outcome. This same power prepares the circumstances and the timing of the events to come in the future. As long as we refrain from interfering with this process, God guides the sequence and brings it to fruition, allowing the end result to enter into time as it is determined by His plan.

God is not in a hurry like we are. He has given us a natural process that requires time, patience, and faith. God was content to take time to create the world and appreciate its goodness at each stage of completion. God was content to allow His people time to experience their own ways and the consequences of these ways before sending His Son for our salvation. God has given us time and a developmental process through which we can grow to maturity. He is content and patient with us as we move through that process as a people and as individuals. It is wise for us to honor His gift of time, His process of development, and His gentleness, even when we do not understand them.

Remember, God's thoughts and ways are not our thoughts and ways (Is. 55:8). Because He is all good and all powerful, we can trust in Him.

As this insight was revealed, my capacity for patience and acceptance was expanded. God paused for a moment in my process, allowing me to absorb both the insight and the personal growth that resulted from it. It was a gift of immeasurable value. Feelings of gratitude poured forth from my heart. God had initiated a transformative process inside me in that moment, and He was not finished yet.

After a period of rest, we moved to the next lesson. God continued to allow me to "see" the process from several different perspectives. I saw how the mystery of the incarnation connects time and eternity, giving us direct access to the power and goodness of God. I saw how the suffering of the cross also connects time and eternity. Through our willingness to suffer, we have the opportunity to pass through the veil that was torn and become one with God through our suffering. These *seeds of insight* would grow in greater fullness and clarity in future meditations.

God's focus shifted once I understood the "big picture" regarding the connection between time and eternity. Now it was time for me to enter into the picture. God made me acutely aware of the desire in my heart. Through that desire He called me forward into union with Him. In that moment the boundaries of my physical form dissolved and I felt as if I had become one with what I had been seeing. I was filled with love. I was surrounded and supported by love. I felt the power of God's love working to heal my past suffering. On an experiential level I understood that through my past efforts in healing I had willingly accepted the cup of suffering for myself, and I had chosen to drink the cup of suffering with others on many occasions. By choosing to participate in the *cup of suffering*, I had also participated in the *cup of blessing*. The suffering was real, and yet, it was consumed by the blessings. I felt healed by the love of God.

Resting in the protection of His embrace, my attention was taken back into an experience in my body – the experience of the terror that had occurred during the events of my abuse. God wanted me to see that there is a choice in the way we deal with suffering. As an infant/child I had no ability to reason, no knowledge of the choice presented in suffering. Propelled by overwhelming fear and natural human instinct, I had learned to escape the confines of my body (the places of devastation and torture) by taking my consciousness out the top of my head through the psychological process known as dissociation.

For years I had lived my life in a partially dissociated state, having very limited access to "owning" my body. It simply wasn't safe down there! Through years of therapy, prayer, and meditation I had learned to live inside myself. Now God was giving me the grace to see that I can make a different choice in my moments of suffering. I can choose love, and desire union with God. That choice brings me forward, helping me to embrace my true identity and the fullness of life. In the past my only choice had been to resist suffering and abandon myself in fear, only to enter into a great abyss that was empty and dreadfully lonely – a void that is beyond description.

As the meditation came to an end, I realized that Mass had ended nearly forty-five minutes earlier. I quickly drew a diagram and jotted down some notes. Then I turned to my husband who had been sitting beside me throughout this process and asked him to listen to the story of my experience. It was an experience that had to be both written and spoken in order to make it real for me. (However, it took several days for the fullness of the experience to "soak in" and be assimilated within me.)

The meditative experience had been overwhelming for me. It seemed as though there should be some sort of ending to bring closure to it. When nothing came to me, I concluded that I must be finished with my prayer for the day. Before leaving the church, however, I paused long enough to scan the readings for Sunday's Mass in celebration of Christ the King, since I was the reader for noon Mass the following day.

In that reading I found the conclusion to this part of the story:

> For thus says the Lord God: "Behold, I myself will search for My sheep and seek them out. As a shepherd cares for his herd in the day when he is among his scattered sheep, so I will care for My sheep and will deliver them from all the places to which they were scattered on a cloudy and gloomy day."
>
> I will feed My sheep and I will lead them to rest, declares the Lord God. I will seek the lost, bring back the scattered, bind up the broken and strengthen the sick; but the sleek and the strong I will destroy. I will feed them with judgment." (Ez. 34: 11-12, 15-16)

At difficult times throughout my suffering I had felt lost, scattered, broken and weak. God found me. He gathered me to Himself. He fed me and allowed me to rest until I became healed and strong.

9

From the Malignant Enemy, Defend Me.

A few days later I was once again captivated by the eternal vision throughout the liturgy of the Eucharist. At the conclusion of the Mass I felt myself being called to the foot of the cross with Jesus. I had spent many hours standing in that very place with my hands resting on the wounds in His feet. I was at peace in this familiar place and ready to participate in any way God had in mind. For quite sometime I simply rested there, grateful for the privilege to be with the Lord in His suffering.

After sometime my heart felt drawn to walk the way of the cross with the Lord. It was a path we had traveled together often. As I rose from the place where I had been kneeling at the altar, I felt different. Deeply immersed in the paschal mystery, I was barely conscious of my connection to my legs and my ability to walk.

Arriving at the first station, my conscious mind was only minimally functional. Weak and unable to genuflect, I simply stood. I acknowledged that Jesus was condemned to death. As I acknowledged the condemnation, it was as if I were present with Him in that moment, and yet, within a split second I was transported *through His memory* back to the garden at Gethsemane. Suddenly there was a *oneness* to the sequence of events that we call the paschal mystery. It was as if I had been swept up into a continuum in which the events that we recognize as being separate and distinct were all contained in one continuous flow.

United with Jesus in His experience in the agony in the garden, I could feel His feelings of anxiety and dread. In His capacity to experience these feelings, He seemed more human to me than during any other time that we had walked together.

Suddenly I knew that He had experienced every human emotion in just the same way that I have experienced them. Emotions have a unique resonant quality, each one being distinct and identifiable. There is an exercise I have used to train my students in recognizing the resonant quality of different feelings, so it was easy for me to become attuned to each feeling our Lord was experiencing as He knelt and prayed at Gethsemane.

First, I recognized that these feelings belonged to Jesus. I then recognized that they had the same resonant quality as the feelings I had experienced when I awaited the torture of ritualistic abuse. During those moments when I waited in silence and despair I knew what was about to happen and that I had no control over it. If I had known how to pray at that young age; I, too, would have asked the Lord: "If it is possible, let this cup pass from me." (Mt. 26:39)

There are moments when we simply know that we are condemned to experience the dreaded events that are about to follow. By the grace of God, I was able to access those feelings from my childhood. Without any thought, feeling, or prayer on my part, the feelings of my childhood experiences were immediately united to Jesus' feelings and thoughts as He suffered the agony in the garden.

I experienced a rush of comfort and consolation that completely consumed my fears, my anxiety, and my dread.

The outpouring of compassion from the heart of God filled me and surrounded me. I felt completely understood, accepted, and loved. Jesus knew my suffering in the most intimate way possible, because He had experienced those same feelings.

I was so overwhelmed by this reality that I felt unable to continue through the stations. Yet, by His grace, I moved through each station in its turn, coming to a deeper and more expanded understanding of my experience of the first station with each successive station I visited.

Fortified by this new understanding of the compassion of God as it is manifested in the action of His Son, I was more effectively able to embrace the cross of my own suffering at the second station. At the third station I could feel that the strength of Jesus presence had been beside me throughout my suffering. Jesus had been with me each time I had fallen. He had been there each time that I needed to cry out for help, and yet, remained silent because of my fear.

As I looked into the face of Mary at the fourth station, I was filled with *a sense of belonging* that cannot be described. She knew about my suffering. She had stood by my side at every moment, ready to offer comfort and consolation when it was over. I experienced hope, knowing that the suffering of my childhood and the memories that haunted me would finally end. She had remained with me throughout the ordeal, and she would continue to be with me. She offered me the same support that she had offered her Son.

Stations five and six reinforced the reality of others who were called by God to support and aid me in my struggle. Simon and Veronica have worn many faces throughout the history of my trials and hardships. Beginning with the early years of my life God sent people like my great-grand-father, my great aunt, and my uncle to be with me and help me persevere through the darkness.

Station seven lifted me up and gave me the strength to endure my experience. Stations eight through eleven are largely a blur in my memory. I only know that the negative impact of the feelings created as a result of the abuse was stripped away from me and nailed to the cross to die.

By the time I reached the twelfth station, I had been transformed in a way that I had never before experienced. I had spent years walking the way of the cross with our Lord, and never had I been so deeply or profoundly touched by the experience. I was attuned to both the humanity and the divinity of Christ. Jesus as true God and true Man had penetrated the depths of my being, bringing His healing balm and soothing a pain so deep that it was beyond my conscious awareness.

The shadow is the place where we hide parts of ourselves that we cannot bear to face. The shame, the loneliness, the terror – all of these things were parts of my history that were beyond my ability to accept and process. Despite the repeated efforts to handle these painful issues throughout the previous fifteen years, there remained a pain – a brokenness that was beyond the human capacity to comprehend, to touch, and to heal.

Only God knows the depth of such pain. In His love for me He sent His son as true God and true Man to fully experience the brokenness *with me* and *for me*. God has never turned away from my pain and brokenness. In His great compassion He has remained with me always, loving and supporting even those parts that I could not bear to acknowledge.

Standing at the twelfth station I realized that Jesus went to prepare a place for me – not only an ultimate resting place in the Kingdom with my Father in heaven, but also a resting place at the foot of the cross where I could unite my wounds to His.

This union of wounds brought healing as I was cleansed by the water flowing from His side and restored to wholeness by the precious blood that accompanies the water. This flowing of blood and water reminded me of the outpouring of God's grace, especially the grace offered to those who pick up their crosses and follow our Lord. My reward is in heaven, and my reward is also at the foot of the cross, where I accept the place He prepared for me.

In all the times I have walked the way of the cross, Jesus has never failed to remind me that He has also prepared a place for me to rest beside Him in the tomb. Before I can stand up and emerge from the tomb, I must rest as Jesus rested, saying to my Father in heaven: "Into your hands I commend my spirit." (Lk. 23:46) This is where my meditation ended for the day. I quietly left the church to go home and rest in the Lord.

This period of rest was important for my ability to more fully integrate an understanding of the power of the blood and water that poured forth from the wounded side of Jesus. Resting in the Lord helped me recall a message He had given me several months earlier. In that message He said that I would be called to endure a period of internal suffering, assuring me that I would be given the grace to suffer. I readily accepted the message because it came to me in late summer, a time of year when I anticipate the recall of events from my childhood. As I continued to rest in the Lord, I remembered the following course of events as they had occurred that fall.

October has always been the most difficult month of the year, since it ends with Halloween – a celebration of death. October holds the memories of countless tortuous events that have haunted my life for the past sixteen years. Episodes from the past come racing into the present, disrupting my life through the recall of extreme terror and memories of abuse. This type of psychological intrusion accompanied by painful body memories is called post-traumatic stress disorder, or PTSD. Because of the repetitious nature of these episodes, I have come to accept their frequent recurrence, knowing that God will be with me and bring forth healing from the pain. "How kind of Him to warn me in advance this time," I thought.

The months to come did bring suffering for me. However, it was somewhat different from past suffering. The psychological intrusions were minimal, while the body memories presented opportunities for self-discovery and healing that were beyond what I had experienced in the past. For about a week prior to the celebration of the Feast of the Lateran Basilica I had endured the intense pain of a urinary tract infection that refused to respond to any kind of treatment. The pain was excruciating, making it very difficult for me to commute to the university, participate in classes, and report to my internship sites. Yet God's grace pulled me through and still enabled me to get to Mass and remain there afterward to pray.

This is the condition in which I found myself on November 9th. By continually remaining close to God, however, I was able to acquire insight and participate in personal growth through my pain and exhaustion.

That day the first reading was from the book of the prophet Ezekiel. The image created by the reading was one of the temple with water flowing from all sides. The image of flowing water immediately grabbed the attention of my mind, causing me to think about the Water Element. According to Chinese theory the Water Element holds memories of old childhood fears. In my effort to integrate the goodness of Chinese medicine with the principles of my Christian faith, I have come to know that a balanced Water Element is life sustaining, and filled with courage and strength, as well as wonder and awe. The reading from Ezekiel, my knowledge of Chinese medicine, my body symptoms, and the time of year were pointing me in a direction toward healing by balancing water.

In my meditation after Mass I offered my experience of water up to God to be blessed. What followed was a spectacular sequence of water images that led me to experience the created beauty of water, and the wonder and awe this created beauty can inspire when we have the grace to appreciate it. (I invite the reader to pray about receiving this *grace to appreciate* as you enter into the following descriptions of nature and the role of water in our lives.)

The meditation began with the image of a huge wall of water immediately to my left. It was being held at bay by the hand of God, yet there was the sense that it could come crushing down at any moment. This image caused me to experience the power of water. The next image was one of immersion in water – something similar to our Lord's baptism in the Jordan. In such a baptismal experience, the person is completely consumed and surrounded, yet they remain whole.

After the experience of immersion, I found myself sitting on the shore, gazing into the water and seeing my reflection. Water has the power to reflect our image and show us who we are. Then I felt as though I had become one with the water. In this oneness, I felt the gentle flow of a stream, an experience that is similar to the flow of God's grace. This flowing water can take various paths. It can create pools of water in which the flow comes to rest. It can move forward, remaining with the flow of existing water, or it can branch off and forge new paths.

I found myself once again as a separate entity from the water, realizing that I had many choices in interacting with its flow. I could become frightened and nearly drown, or I could trust in the supportive quality of the water and learn to float. I could also go wherever the water took me, or I could swim against the current. In this choice I could learn acceptance and cooperation, or I could find strength in swimming up stream. In going with the flow I could also find myself in rapidly flowing whitewater where I could learn the skill of navigation.

After participating in this *dance with water*, I once again found myself sitting on the shore. Here I realized the cleansing and soothing affects of water as it flowed over my feet and legs. This image of the shoreline also allowed me to appreciate the ability of water to approach and recede in its contact with the shore. Off in the distance, however, there was the majesty of the waves as they swelled and came crashing down against the rock.

The final image of water was one of a gentle rain from heaven which waters the earth and brings forth life – rain that fills our rivers and streams, providing drinking water to quench our thirst.

Filled with the extraordinary beauty of water, I remained seated in the pew, drinking in the wonder and awe of the experience. I felt as though I were floating, completely supported and sustained by the life-giving properties of water.

After resting in the Lord for some time, I felt the urge to pray the stations. The feelings of wonder and awe remained with me as I moved to the first station. My recall of the personal healing experience that followed is sketchy at best; however, it provides an overall understanding of the transformation that was accomplished by this vision.

The first station created a paradoxical experience. I was filled with joy as I entered into the reality of Jesus being condemned to death. It was like being able to experience the delight in the heart of God as He was filled with anticipation during this event that was going to seal salvation history. Reflecting now on experiencing joy at Jesus being condemned to death seems bizarre, but at the time it felt entirely appropriate.

The second station allowed me to experience simultaneous realities. I was aware of both time and eternity. There were equal measures of joy and sorrow as Jesus embraced His cross. Joy was associated with the eternal reality, and sorrow was connected with the historical event. The third station was filled with wisdom – the wisdom in the mind of Christ and the wisdom of God on high. I was filled with the beauty of water, the joy of God, and the wisdom of Christ. This experience was one of such great fullness that it is far beyond the power of mere words to describe it.

Then I met Mary on the way of the cross. It was as if God turned me over to her tender care to help me with the remaining stations. Suddenly I recalled the most intense fears of my childhood abuse – a fear that is marked by threats to cut my tongue out, if I spoke of the abuse.

In the midst of the goodness that God was allowing me to experience, all of my deep-seated childhood fears began to emerge. I experienced the holding patterns that these fears had created in my body. I experienced the terror that remained imprinted on my physical tissue. I felt how the intensity of these feelings had propelled my consciousness to escape my body and go out through the top of my head.

As I continued to walk the way of the cross, my fears emerged and were dissipated, like the ebb and flow of the tide. God set me free from them, and He healed me. My fears were nailed to the cross and they died, when Jesus died for me. Parts of me that had been lost, stolen, and abandoned were returned to me and allowed to find their natural resting place. The old route I used to escape from my body during times of intense fear was sealed and I was made whole on yet another level.

With a much greater awareness of how God protected me from the malignant enemy, I rested in His goodness and love.

10

At the Hour of My Death, Call Me. And Bid Me Come to You. That with Your Saints I May Praise You. For Everlasting Ages. Amen.

Having mentally recapped the events of the fall season, I was ready to bring closure to my exploration of the mystery of suffering. I sensed that the process was nearing completion, and yet, I struggled to articulate it. My journal for the first Sunday of Advent read:

> *Each time I sit with the Lord to review the meditation and record the process, there is a struggle similar to the birthing of a child. At times the exhaustion and the frustrated efforts to understand loom before me like huge obstacles in my path. If not for the burning desire that glows like an eternal flame in my heart, I would submit to my own lack of perseverance and set the project aside.*

It is that flame of eternal desire that prods my heart to remain open and my mind to continually search for the truth. There are times when God calls me to rest and be restored, and there are times when He urges me to go on despite my protests and my defeatist attitude. In this present effort, as with countless times in my past, He refuses to let me quit. There is an important message to be shared, a message that must come from one who knows His Son as the Suffering Servant.

Through the flame of eternal desire God ignites and enlivens my weak human will by uniting it to His will. This enables me to say: "Thy will be done." So often in my young life I was silenced and prevented from speaking – silenced by an ignorance of my faith – silenced by threats to my life and my will – silenced by the failure of others to recognize the gifts I had to share. Now God will no longer allow me to be silenced. The time for silence has past. This is the time for me to share my story and bear witness to Christ, so that others might know the love of God and be healed.

Before I began to write today, I struggled in a darkness that was vast and empty. Not knowing where or how to begin this section that concludes the mystery of suffering, I prayed to Jesus as the Alpha and the Omega, the beginning and the end. He did not immediately come to my aid. Instead, He allowed me to struggle in frustration. Feeling lost like a sheep gone astray, I continued to offer everything to God for His blessing, asking Him to enlighten me and guide me on my way. "Of all the mysteries of your life and all the words of sacred Scripture, where do I begin, Lord?" I cried out.

He responded: "Go to Cana in Galilee, to the wedding feast." There I heard the words of Mary: "Do whatever He tells you." (Jn. 2:5) I sat reading and waiting to comply with her message, and still no word. Finally the inspiration came to read the 53rd chapter of Isaiah about the Suffering Servant. So many words touched me as I read it. I had no idea which words God wanted me to choose to begin the meditation. "Read until I tell you to stop," were the words I heard. I continued to read chapter 53 over and over until I stopped at the seventh verse:

> *Though he was harshly treated, he submitted, and opened not his mouth; Like a lamb led to the slaughter or a sheep before its shearers, he was silent and opened not his mouth. (Is. 53:7)*

This is where the last leg of my journey began – in silence, the silence of those who are oppressed and afflicted. This is a painful silence that harbors many wounds – a silence that often prevents healing of those wounds. It requires great courage to enter into such a silence and reveal the pain that has been concealed for so many years.

Several years ago I wrote a rather lengthy paper addressing wounds and how they are healed. My mother could not bring herself to read it. My father was barely able to respond to its content, saying only how remarkable it was for anyone to have such an understanding of wounds. For a brief time I think he actually had a glimpse of how intensely painful my life has been. My parents have a long history of lacking authentic compassion, and avoiding responsibility for inflicting pain on others. They have spent a lifetime engaged in "the blame game." This became evident to me in my adulthood, when a friend commented to me: "You know, Jenny, everything that goes wrong is *not* your fault."

It has taken years of building healthy relationships and hearing supportive, encouraging comments from others to let go of old beliefs about myself that simply were not true, beliefs that often become attached to the family member who is burdened with the role of scapegoat. An even greater burden was placed on me by my own struggle to follow the commandment: "Honor your father and your mother." My faith presented other obstacles to my healing, when my family members used that faith in a manipulative way to reinforce their own position and coerce me to conform to their ways. Speaking out and expressing the truth was seen by them as being *unchristian*. I suppose they are unaware of how Christ spoke out against the moneychangers in the temple. Sometimes people are called to speak the truth, regardless of how painful it may be, or how much upheaval it may cause.

Often when Jesus spoke in the Gospels, it was to teach or preach or heal. He knew there were times to speak. He was aware of the different ways in which words could be spoken. He knew that the words needed to be heard.

He also knew that there were times to remain silent. Those times could be used for prayer, recalling His relationship to the Father. Those times were also used to establish an intimate relationship with those of us who would suffer oppression and affliction – those who would suffer in silence.

Jesus' moments of silence were a great gift to all of us who suffered (and continue to suffer) in silence. Through silence we find union with Him. Through that union we are strengthened and encouraged to speak the truth. Courage comes to us in Jesus' own words to Pilate before He began the way of the cross: "For this I have been born, and for this I have come into the world, to testify to the truth. Everyone who is of the truth hears My voice." (Jn. 18:37)

Throughout the remainder of my life I will be called to speak the truth. May I have the courage to speak the truth until the hour of my death, when He calls me home. Amen.

Part II

Part I described my personal journey with God, high-lighting my healing through my relationship with Him. This was only one facet of my journey – the facet that was responsible for bringing me hope and ultimate wholeness. Part I described the supernatural journey that was guided by my dependence on God.

Part II is quite different in its orientation. It focuses on the frustration I experienced in my earthly journey toward healing. I say toward healing because there were efforts made in that direction, but the results were less than satis-factory when they were attempted without the guidance of God's grace. Decades of frustration were turned into hope through my pursuit of complementary medicine – a journey that was guided by God's grace and fueled by my perseverance.

11

Frustration Turns to Hope

Listen, for I will speak noble things;
and the opening of my lips will reveal right things.
For my mouth will utter truth. (Pv. 8:6-7)

Being called to speak the truth can be a heavy burden. Those who speak the truth must have extraordinary courage and access to wisdom. Only when wisdom is the message can authentic truth be spoken. Wisdom accumulates over time as we gain *knowledge* from intellectual endeavors and *understanding* from our experience. However, we can spend countless hours accumulating knowledge and years learning through our experience, and still fail to achieve the wisdom that guides us in making right choices. How can that be?

The letter of James compares *earthly wisdom* with *wisdom from above.* James describes wisdom from above as "first of all pure, then peaceable, gentle, compliant, full of mercy and good fruits, without inconstancy or insincerity" (Jam. 3:17). This was the wisdom that guided me in my relationship with God as it was described in Part I. This was the wisdom that I eventually came to know and trust. It is dramatically different from the wisdom I had received in my childhood, or the wisdom I encountered when I sought help for my pain from traditional sources.

Human beings often operate through earthly wisdom – wisdom that James describes as being unspiritual, and based on bitter jealousy and selfish ambition. This disposition leads individuals to make choices based on either fear or pride, instead of relying on humble confidence in God. Hearts that are governed by jealousy and selfish ambition promote an environment of competition in which participants either win or lose. Hearts that are guided by humble confidence in the Lord are attuned to wisdom and compassion. Wisdom is the sign of an open mind and compassion is the sign of an open heart. In the early years of my life wisdom and compassion were not part of my healing process. I was lost in a world of limited knowledge and mere human wisdom, and I was constantly on the losing end of the battle.

My intimate knowledge of pain and suffering began in the early years of my childhood, sometime before the age of ten. I have no recollection of living pain-free in the early part of my life. My suffering was further complicated because my father refused to acknowledge any type of pain or suffering. According to him, pain and illness were *all in your head*. A few examples will help to clarify this point. I started to work in the stores when I was eight years old. *Never* was it permissible to miss a day of work. He had a similar attitude toward attending school. In his mind there were things to be done and goals to be accomplished – his goals. These goals did not permit taking time off.

The most painful recollection I have regarding his strict guidelines for duty and obedience occurred when I was 17 years old. My parents enjoyed vacationing in Florida during the winter. That year they had assigned me the task of caring for my three younger siblings while they were gone. However, prior to their departure I was stricken with a severe case of mononucleosis. The doctor said I had a "text-book case of mono," but he could not confirm it with a blood test. I was so weak and exhausted that I could barely function. My parents chose to go to Florida and leave me with the responsibility of taking care of my siblings.

Every day I got up and took my brother and two sisters to school before going to the doctor's office to get a vitamin B12 shot and then returning to school. After several days of this routine, my math teacher – a gruff, demanding woman – called me into the hall and said, "I am sending you home, and I don't want to see you in my class until you are well." I left school and returned to the doctor's office. I signed in with the receptionist and took a seat in the waiting room. Within seconds a woman I referred to as "Nurse Hatchet" (because she was usually very mean) came out to the waiting room, picked me up in her arms and carried me back to a treatment room. On the way back she said to me, "We have to get you out of there. You're bad for business!" She was actually joking with me, trying to make light of a very bad situation.

The doctor took a blood sample once again. This time it was positive, indicating a severe case of mononucleosis. The doctor called my parents in Florida and told them they had to come home. I was in bed for months, often uncon-scious. I missed the remainder of my junior year in high school. My parents did come home, feeling somewhat guilty for what they had done. Their act of reparation included two dresses from Florida, but no change in their behavior.

This is an example of the lack of support that I experi-enced from my family regarding my bout with mono. It is a difficult and painful story to tell, and it is the truth. I realize now that the physical pain that filled my body, as well as the emotional pain and dysfunction I experienced, was directly related to the way I was treated by my family.

The sense of hopelessness and frustration regarding my family situation contributed to my chronic pain. In turn, the chronic pain fueled my sense of hopelessness and frustration because there seemed to be no relief. Traditional medicine offered only the *illusion* of help. My general practitioner was a very caring and compassionate man who referred me to other practitioners, but no one had the tools to help me. I endured torturous tests that revealed nothing. I tolerated more accusations: "It's all in your head." I was told that I would have to "learn to live with the pain."

One well-meaning doctor suggested that I see a psychiatrist. The psychiatrist requested a family session to include me and both of my parents. Once again, I was old enough to drive, and therefore, responsible for taking myself to the appointment. I was the only one who attended the session, explaining to the doctor that my dad had to work and my mother had to take the dog to the vet. The psychiatrist was noticeably irritated and informed me that I was not the one with the problem. This session resulted in a letter from the psychiatrist to my parents. After reading the letter, my father claimed that the psychiatrist knew nothing. My mother declared that the psychiatrist *blamed* my father, and, of course, she had known all along that it was his fault. There were no more visits to the psychiatrist.

In subsequent years I had additional visits with other counselors. By and large, they were no more fruitful than the one described above. In short, rather than being a source of support and encouragement, my family was a source of my symptoms. No help was available through traditional medical routes, nor through counseling. It was as though I was doomed to live a life of severe chronic pain.

There were many occasions when that burden seemed worse than being condemned to death. At least death meant that the suffering would end in the near future versus the prospect of living with that awful pain for decades. There were times that were filled with helplessness, hopelessness, and despair. The pain was overwhelming, and the thought of having no relief was often unbearable.

Allow me to simply name the factors that contributed to the layered effect of my pain:

- *There were two severe blows to the head before the age of 10, causing distortion in the bones of the head. The first head trauma occurred when I was 5 years old. My sled went out of control on the ice, and I hit the corner of my grandparent's stone house with the center of my forehead. The second head trauma occurred in a bomb shelter in the 1960's. I was about 10 years old. As I was playing with a small group of girls in the top bunk, they held my hands behind my back and tickled me. I fell out of the bed head first and landed on the center of my forehead once again. Since that time I have come to understand that such traumas can only be corrected through craniosacral therapy.*

- *There was a severe tearing of my pelvis in a toboggan accident at the age of 22. Afterward I was in shock and unable to walk for several hours. A variety of treatments were required to correct the problems related to this accident, among them were chiropractic care, neuromuscular therapy, movement therapy, and treatments with the cold laser and the percussor.*

- *The pain and dysfunction of my family life was stored in the tissue of my body. The key elements in my recovery were prayer and meditation, along with process work, bodywork, and essential oils.*

- *The memories of the abuse were stored in my unconscious mind, and from that distant place they reached into my body to cause gripping pain. Once again, prayer and meditation played a critical role in my healing, as did bodywork, process work, chiropractic care, essential oils, and flower essences.*

- *Endometriosis filled my abdominal cavity, causing my uterus to adhere to my bladder and my colon. This condition went undiagnosed for over 20 years. Recently, at the age of 49 I had a hysterectomy. It was one of the few medical interventions that brought relief. (Most of the conditions listed here were successfully treated with some form of complementary medicine: bodywork, process work, chiropractic care, nutrition, herbs, vitamins, minerals, essential oils, flower essences, meditation, prayer, movement therapy, exercise, and treatments with a percussor and a cold laser. These were things that I discovered on my own in the past 18 years.)*

- *I was plagued by interstitial cystitis, a condition that feels like a chronic bladder infection. Medicine brought some relief for this condition, after suffering without help for over 30 years. Greater relief was achieved through the use of essential oils, nutrition and supplements.*

- *I suffered from a series of food allergies, including many grains, dairy products, and legumes. Before discovering that I had allergies, I ate all of these foods. By removing them from my diet and adding them back to the diet one at a time, I was able to determine the specific reaction of each food and confirm the need to eliminate it from my diet. Through this process I came to understand that chronic muscle aches and joint pains can result from food allergies, especially foods such as wheat and corn. In the case of food allergies, no intervention will bring long-term relief until the allergen is no longer ingested.*

For years there was pain in every inch of my body. I could not tolerate being touched. Nothing provided relief, except the mild, short-term relief I received from aerobic exercise. The pain was incomprehensible to me and to others. No one understood, and no one was able to help me for years. That is why the relief that came to me during my pregnancy was such a tremendous gift. However, it was short-lived. The pain returned after Lauren was born. At that time, the pain actually began to escalate as my anxiety concerning my grandfather grew and body memories began to stir. The exhaustion, resulting from extended periods without sleep, was also a major contributing factor.

Physically, mentally, emotionally, and spiritually, I was approaching a time of crisis. God was allowing me to begin to see what was contributing to my pain, because the time had come for me to be healed. The wheels of divine providence had set the process in motion. One by one pieces of insight would expand my understanding, as new opportunities for healing were presented in my environment. God truly never gives us more than we can handle, even though our present experiences may seem to be overwhelming. His grace is always with us to guide the process. All that is required of us is that we depend on Him.

Before Lauren reached her first birthday, the pain had escalated to a debilitating level. One morning while I was exercising in the bedroom, I collapsed on the floor with pain so severe that I could barely move. Fortunately, Lauren was in her walker and safe from harm for the moment. As usual, my husband was playing golf and would be gone for hours. With nearly every muscle in my body screaming in spasm, I rolled onto my stomach and began to creep toward the phone. With each painful movement I resisted the overwhelming urge to scream or moan, fearing that these sounds would frighten Lauren. It seemed to take forever for me to travel a few feet to reach the nearby table where the phone was located. Grabbing at the dangling cord, I pulled until the phone fell off the table. I called the country club and explained: "You have to send someone to get my husband. Tell him there's an emergency, and he must come home immediately."

Without hanging up the phone, I curled into a fetal position and sobbed quietly with tears pouring down my face. That is how my husband found me when he arrived home. He was unable to move me, or even touch me because the pain was so severe. At my request he called our general practitioner who offered to come to the house. The doctor gave me a series of cortisone injections, and they put me in bed. Before falling asleep I recall hearing the doctor say, "That was enough cortisone to treat a horse."

When I awoke later that day I had one compelling thought: I need to call a man named Paul St. John and find out how I can see him as soon as possible. I did not know Paul St. John. I simply knew of him. Several weeks before my pain crisis, our family had been in Florida visiting my dad. This annual visit to Florida had occurred for years. During each visit I would make an appointment for a massage at the Boca Hotel and Club – every year with the same massage therapist. That year she was away, and a young woman was "filling in" for her.

A miraculous thing happened as a result of that massage – I actually felt some relief from my pain, and it lasted for several days. During my massage I commented on her different technique, and how it was making me feel. She explained that she was *in training* as a neuromuscular therapist with Paul St. John. She had only attended two courses, and yet she was able to give me some *relief* from my pain, and more importantly *hope*. She was kind enough to write down Paul St. John's name and the city in Florida where his clinic was located. I tucked that piece of paper in my wallet and took it back to Altoona with me, thinking that I would contact him the next time I planned to go to Florida.

Clearly, God wanted me to contact him sooner. Moving slowly and carefully, I got up from the bed and found my wallet. There it was – the paper that represented hope for my recovery. I would have called him in that moment, but it was the Saturday of Labor Day weekend. I waited until the following Tuesday morning to call. I had two questions to ask: Where is he? And how can I see him? I was amazed to learn that he was teaching a seminar in Baltimore – only three hours away – the following weekend. His secretary asked if I wanted to attend, and I responded with a resounding, "Yes!"

In a flurry of activity I prepared to attend the seminar. During the few days that followed I had an appointment with my chiropractor. When he learned about my trip, he strongly encouraged me to approach Paul as soon as I registered at the seminar because the presenter often takes people from the audience to use for demonstration. From that point forward, I was a woman on a mission.

When I arrived at the seminar location, I sought out the people in charge and presented my case. They took me to meet Paul. He did a preliminary evaluation on me, and suggested that I consider being his *demo model* throughout the weekend. I agreed without reservation, and my journey of healing began.

Throughout the weekend I received Neuromuscular Therapy on the various muscles of my shoulder girdle.

Each time Paul found one of the many trigger points in my muscles, I winced with pain as tears rolled down my face. Then within seconds of receiving his masterful touch, the pain began to subside as the muscle tissue released. At the end of the first day I was exhausted from receiving bodywork from Paul, and then participating in the trading process with my partner. Co-mingled with the exhaustion were feelings of exhilaration. The burden was being lifted. I was being set free from the pain. Throughout the night I lay awake in bed overcome with wonder and awe, realizing that I had been relieved of a tremendous amount of pain, and yet, knowing that we had barely scratched the surface.

The events of the second day touched me very deeply on both a mental and an emotional level. The other people who were attending the seminar had begun to know me and understand the story of my suffering. I could feel the compassion in their hearts as they watched me receiving the work from Paul. Many of them came up to hug me, and to thank me for sharing my pain with them because it helped them appreciate the powerful results of Neuromuscular Therapy. The support and encouragement they offered was foreign to me, and yet, I was able to accept it because it was so genuine. It helped me to heal the deep emotional wounds that I had sustained in previous years. Fifty strangers *heard* what I had been trying to communicate for decades. They *understood* my pain and had the courage to enter it with me. They helped me acknowledge my pain and move through it. Because of their compassion I experienced greater wholeness.

Throughout the day Paul hovered around me, making sure that I was okay. He spent a good deal of time watching me work with others and showing me how to improve my skills. He knew that I had no prior training or experience in providing bodywork. While watching me work on another student during the afternoon session, he paused and looked directly into my eyes and said, "You really should consider doing this work. You're a natural."

Paul was the first of many of my teachers to recognize the gift I had been given by God to heal others. During the months that followed my first encounter with bodywork, I received numerous private sessions with Paul and the staff at his clinic in Florida. I also attended the remaining workshops that he offered, and became certified in Neuromuscular Therapy.

One important finding that Paul shared with me during my sessions was his concern about the condition of the bones in my head. The occiput is the bone at the base of the skull. It should be level from left to right. My occiput was about an inch different from side to side. He said that his ability to help me would be limited unless I received some Craniosacral Therapy.

Through a series of referrals I was eventually seen by John Upledger, DO and founder of the Upledger Institute. My improvement was dramatic. As a result I began taking courses through the Institute, progressing through the second level of advanced training with Dr. Upledger. Through my connection with the Upledger Institute, I was introduced to and trained by: Bonnie Bainbridge Cohen, founder of the School for Bodymind Centering; Dr. Fritz Smith, originator of Zero Balancing; and Dr. Aminah Raheem, originator of Process Acupressure. My education in the various aspects of complementary medicine has continued to this day. It has included training in the use of nutritional supplements, essential oils, flower essences, biofeedback, neurolinguistic programming, and equipment such as the percussor, the adjuster, and the cold laser. As I discovered things that were beneficial to me in my own healing journey, I studied them and learned to use the skills that would help others. My pain and suffering led me on a journey that facilitated my own healing, and it helped me to develop the gift of healing that God had given to me.

For about 15 years I eagerly absorbed knowledge, mastered various skills, and practiced healing protocols. I depended on God to send me the people He had chosen for me to help. Through daily prayer and meditation God took me beyond the simple process of healing that used the protocols I had learned from others. Because I believed that each time I touched a human body I was touching the wisdom of God, *He called me into that wisdom* and helped me to see the underlying models of healing that contribute to individual wholeness and well-being.

Most of the models are simple geometric shapes that become rich with wisdom when they are connected to the power and order of creation through the human body. The human body is the pinnacle of the created order because it is created in God's own image. The very wisdom of God is contained within each human form. By using my hands to touch literally hundreds of human bodies, I was able to connect with the wisdom of God as it is manifested in the body. Over time, a series of models developed. I noticed that these models were repeated over and over. They had a universal application. They provided a general framework into which the stories of individual people could take root and come to life, producing greater understanding and acceptance of their life circumstances.

These models became the foundation of my therapy sessions. As I would listen to the struggles of individual clients, a model – or healing image – would enter my mind. After the client had completed the story, I would explain the model that related to the circumstances that the client had described. Then, if necessary, I would share a personal story to demonstrate how I had used the model to find healing. Often the models themselves were so clear that the client required nothing more than the healing image. As soon as the clients achieved an understanding of how the model related to them, a light would radiate from behind their faces. They would experience a sense of *knowing* that was beyond description. I would witness this same *glowing signal of understanding* when I would use the models as teaching tools in classroom situations.

Although some of the models are based on the human body and its functioning, most of them are based on fundamental geometric shapes. Some are based on lines and some are based on circles. Each model is unique and has a special application in the healing process. I have compiled these models in a two volume series where they are described in greater fullness.

Volume I is entitled, "We are Called." It describes the linear models of healing. Each linear model is presented along with a description of the model, and a story to facilitate an understanding of how the model can be used. The book describes a collection of *horizontal* linear models that facilitate an understanding of struggles between opposites, and ways to find balance by becoming centered in Christ. The *vertical* linear models help individuals navigate the journey home – the vertical ascent – toward God.

Volume II describes models that are based on the circle. Some models are cyclical, some are spherical, and others are in the shape of a spiral or a series of concentric circles. Each model contains unique elements that direct the process of healing. For example, the cyclical model highlights the seasons of the year, both the seasons of nature and the seasons of the liturgical year. One year can be seen as a circle, while multiple years can be viewed as a spiral. Each year provides special opportunities for developmental growth and healing. Those opportunities accumulate over the years, giving us a chance to grow in wisdom and love.

I was perfectly content to continue using these models for healing, teaching, and spiritual direction. I believed that I was doing the work to which God had called me. However, in God's plan for my life there was more. To my utter amazement all of the doors that sustained my practice for healing and teaching in Altoona closed, when the city of Altoona decided that the building that I was temporarily using for my business was no longer suitable to be used as a school. In addition, plans that I had made to build a new facility in a nearby area fell through. This was a shocking reality for me, and yet, I believe that when God closes one door, He opens another. The door that stood wide open for me led to Franciscan University in Steubenville, Ohio. God called me to return to school to acquire a master's degree in counseling.

I truly believed that God had called me to attend Franciscan University. I saw my instructors as His instruments to further my education and my development as a healer. I viewed each assignment for class as an assignment from God. I offered them up to be guided by His grace.

God was most present with me during my courses in Christian counseling. There were things He wanted me to know and understand about Christian counseling. In many respects, the field of counseling remains largely secular in its orientation. Even those who practice Christian counseling often use models that are based on secular theories of counseling. There is no unified Christian model that can be used. In fact, there remains considerable resistance to the notion of Christian counseling. Consequently, my professor assigned us the task of writing a paper entitled, "The Need for Christian Counseling."

The process of writing this paper solidified my own thoughts on Christian counseling, and opened *my eyes* to the "need for Christian counseling." Because of its transformative power, I am including this paper as the following chapter in this book.

I invite the reader to review the paper with an eager mind and an open heart. Allow Jesus to teach you as He taught me. May He bless you richly as you read.

12

The Need for Christian Counseling

See to it that no one captivate you with an empty,
seductive philosophy
according to human tradition,
according to the elemental powers of the world and
not according to Christ. (Col. 2:8)

A Societal Need for Christian Counseling

In his book, *How Now Shall We Live?*, Charles Colson
shares the view of Samuel Huntingdon, a distinguished
Harvard scholar, stating that "the world is divided not so
much by geographic boundaries as by religious and cultural traditions, by people's most deeply held beliefs – by
worldviews." Colson goes on to state that "Christians
would agree. Because we are religious creatures, our lives
are defined by our ultimate beliefs more sharply than any
other factor" (1999, p.19).

If our lives are defined so sharply by these "ultimate beliefs," it is important to ask: what are these beliefs and how do they impact our lives? Colson proposes that:

> ... *every worldview can be analyzed by the way it answers three basic questions: Where did we come from and who are we (creation)? What has gone wrong with the world (fall)? And what can we do to fix it (redemption)? These three questions form a grid that we can use to break down the inner logic of every belief system or philosophy that we encounter (1999, p.14).*

From a Christian perspective our worldview tells us that we were created by a transcendent and loving God. We were created to be in relationship with Him – called to know, love, and serve Him. We also believe that early in our history we defied God and as a result of our behavior, we became separated from Him – an event known as *the fall*. We believe that God in His abundant mercy then sent His only Son to die for us, so that we might be restored in our relationship with our Father in heaven. Thus, in love we were created, in justice we were condemned, and in mercy we were redeemed.

This forms the basis of the Christian worldview. This is the philosophy that we embrace according to Christ. It is the philosophy that we are called to live, while rejecting the "empty, seductive philosophy according to human tradition, according to the elemental powers of the world" (Col.2:8). When we live according to our Christian philosophy, we are said to have an *intrinsic* religious faith. According to social psychologist Gordon Allport, this strong faith is the principal motivating force in people's lives. Their faith impacts their everyday behavior and decisions. This intrinsic faith is characterized by a close personal relationship with God. (This can be contrasted with people who possess *extrinsic* faith and merely use religion to obtain some non-spiritual goal.)

The distinction between intrinsic and extrinsic faith is an important one when we consider the relationship between religion and a sense of well-being. Harold G. Koenig, M.D. has been studying the impact that people's faith has on their health and well-being since the mid-1980s. Dr. Koenig is certified in family medicine, psychiatry, geriatric medicine, and geriatric psychiatry. As the director of Duke University's Center for the Study of Religion/Spirituality and Health he studied a geriatric population in the mid-west. After statistical analysis, he concluded "that religious faith, level of intrinsic religiosity, and worship patterns such as church attendance were important parts of these people's lives and probably contributed to their improved emotional and physical health" (1999, p.35-36).

Dr. Koenig reported that "many of the Duke Center's studies have produced ground breaking findings" (1999, p.23). The following list is a selected summary of these findings.

- *People with strong religious faith are less likely to suffer depression from stressful life events, and if they do, they are more likely to recover from depression than those who are less religious.*

- *The deeper a person's religious faith, the less likely he or she is to be crippled by depression during and after hospitalization for physical illness.*

- *Religious people have healthier lifestyles. They tend to avoid alcohol and drug abuse, risky sexual behavior, and other unhealthy habits.*

- *People who attend religious services regularly have stronger immune systems than their less religious counterparts.*

- *Religious people live longer. The risk of dying from all causes is up to 35% lower for people who attend religious services at least once a week than for those who attend less frequently (1999, p.24).*

In addition to the above findings from the Duke Center's studies, Charles Colson reports a staggering list of benefits from the growing body of scientific evidence. In *How Now Shall We Live?* Colson shares, among other things, the following findings.

- *There is a strong correlation between participation in religious activities and the avoidance of crime.*

- *Persons who do not attend church are four times more likely to commit suicide than those who attend church frequently.*

- *Church attendance is the most important predictor of marital stability. In fact, churchgoers are more likely to say they would marry the same spouse again – an important measure of marital satisfaction.*

- *Religion has also shown itself to be an important factor in preventing teen sexual relations, babies born out of wedlock, discord between parent and child, and other forms of family breakdown (1999, p.311-12).*

Religion appears to be a strong grounding and stabilizing force for adolescents as well as adults. In *The Healing Power of Faith* Koenig recaps the 1995 findings of psychologists Donahue and Benson in their comprehensive and thorough review of "accumulated research on the relationship between religion and adolescent mental health" (1999, p.129). The research studied a representative sample of 34,129 young people, more than half of whom stated that religion played an important part in their lives.

The researchers found that religion was "positively associated" with emotionally healthy values and socially accepted behavior. ... Religious students were less likely to harbor suicidal thoughts or to make actual attempts on their lives. These religious students also showed significantly lower levels of drug and alcohol abuse, premature sexual involvement, and criminal delinquency. In other words, religion appeared to protect a highly representative sampling of young people from the negative affects of an increasingly stressful adolescence in America (1999, p.129).

Donahue and Benson concluded that: "Religion has some manifestly positive effects on behavior. ... When it comes to a wide variety of at-risk behaviors that are concerns to people who work with youth, religion works; it should be allowed more space to do so" (1999, p. 103).

The research findings reported above take on even greater significance when we learn that 96% of people in the U.S. believe in God or a universal power; 90% pray; and 43% regularly attend religious services. Thus, according to the poles many Americans are religious, and they take their religion seriously.

With such a clearly demonstrated need for religion, and such compelling evidence to support the positive impact that faith has on our mental and physical health, as well as our sense of well-being; what prevents us from adequately addressing the faith needs of our clients in counseling sessions? More than likely, it is related to the

... conventional wisdom among psychiatrists and psychologists, handed down from Sigmund Freud, the founder of psychoanalysis, who defined religion

as *"a universal obsessional neurosis," "an infantile
helplessness," and "regression to primary narcis-
sism."* The terminology has changed since Freud,
but most psychologists and psychiatrists retain the
assumption that religion is a negative factor in
mental health and that it is associated with mental
pathologies (Colson, 1999).

Colson goes on to state that the new scientific data clearly
shows that:

... *if we ignore biblical principles, we end up living
in ways that run against the grain of our being,
and we pay a steep price in terms of stress, depression, family conflict, and even physical illness.
Rather than being an arbitrary set of rules and re-
strictions that repress and distort our true nature,
Christianity actually describes our true nature and
shows us how to live with it (1999, p.315).*

What is the wise and prudent choice? Should we continue to ignore or minimize the religious/spiritual aspects
of our clients based on the opinion of Freud and those who
have blindly followed his religious bias? Or should we tap
the wisdom from recent scientific studies concerning the
truth of the relationship between religion and well-being?
Perhaps an examination of the process of counseling will
provide further clarification.

A Personal Need for Christian Counseling

Colson suggests that "our major task in life is to discover what is true and to live in step with that truth" (1999, p.14). Discovering what is true and learning to live in step with that truth is an ongoing process through which we come to understand our authentic human needs and choose healthy ways to meet those needs within the framework of our Christian identity.

As this process unfolds, we learn about our lifestyle and the consequences of the choices we make. We learn about the process of development and the things that facilitate this process according to our Christian beliefs, as well as the obstacles that stand in the way.

In conjunction with this process, we experience the mental conflicts and resulting anxiety, as well as the emotional confusion and stress. In addition, there are often times in our human weakness when we experience being abandoned by God. We have difficulty interpreting the events of our lives in light of the beliefs that we hold dear. We notice dysfunctional patterns in our own lives, in our relationships, and in society. We struggle because we are in the world, yet we are *not of the world*. How do we define and live this process of growth as Christians? How do we learn the will of God and find resignation with it? How do we resolve the conflicts we notice both within ourselves and in the world?

These are all issues and concerns that Christians bring into the counseling process because of their worldview. They are issues and concerns that are *not* adequately addressed because many counselors are divorced from religious beliefs or hold the opinion that religious beliefs should not be part of the counseling process. As a result of the evolution of counseling, the basic process that provides its foundation is at best devoid of religion and at worst hostile to it. Given such a climate, how can Christians have their counseling needs met?

I propose that a secular approach to counseling can be quite frustrating to a Christian. The underlying reason is the difference in fundamental beliefs. Both secular counseling and the process of Christian growth focus on the development of the *self*. From this single point of similarity they diverge dramatically. *In Psychology as Religion: The Cult of Self-Worship* Paul Vitz discusses the most influential self-theorists, including Fromm, Rogers, Maslow, and May. In Vitz' opinion each of the theorists made a unique contribution to "self-theory." For example, in Maslow's hierarchy of needs, the ultimate level to which one ascends is self-actualization. On a superficial level we may ask: "What is wrong with that?"

Vitz goes on to quote Maslow's description of the essential quality of these "self-actualized types:"

> *A few centuries ago these would all have been described as men who walk in the path of God or as godly men. A few say that they believe in God, but describe this God more as a metaphysical concept than as a personal figure. If religion is defined only in social-behavioral terms, then these are all religious people, the atheist included. But if more conservatively we use the term religion so as to include and stress the supernatural element and institutional orthodoxy (certainly the more common usage) then our answer must be quite different, for then none of them is religious (1977, p.24).*

Hence, the self-theorists hold that "man's God is man." Man is to achieve his full potential, self-actualization, strictly through his own efforts. They deny the importance of God and religion. This is at odds with the Christian belief in a transcendent God – a belief that is beautifully expressed by Jones and Butman in *Modern Psychotherapies* as they discuss the beliefs of Kierkegaard, the "father of existentialism." According to Jones and Butman, Kierkegaard

> ... *believed that the only genuine and true decisions that could be made about becoming a self had to be made transparently before and in relationship with God. The very idea of autonomously choosing what sort of self to become, with no recourse to the one in whom we have our being (the essence of secular existentialism), was anathema to the thought of Kierkegaard. Second, because we are to make our choices of who to become in the context of our relationship with God, it is clear that there is definitely a self that I am to become, a "true self" that I am to actualize by making the "right" choices. Our personhood is not wholly "plastic," moldable to any shape, as many existentialist thinkers today would assert. Rather, we are to become the people that God would hold out for us to become (1991, p.281).*

These two opposing views cannot be reconciled. They create two entirely different ways of relating to people. Paul Vitz describes these as relating to a *person* vs. an *individual*. Vitz' article entitled "A Christian Theory of Personality" appears in *The Nature and Tasks of a Personalist Psychology*. In this article he summarizes the difference between a person and an individual as follows.

A *person* is created by God in the image of God.

An *individual* is created by the self in the image of the self.

A *person* loves and trusts God, and loves others as the self; persons forgive those who have hurt them.

An *individual* loves and trusts the self, trusts others, and rejects or ignore God; individuals forget those who have hurt them.

A *person* has the goal of committed relationships with others, and a state of union with God.

An *individual* has the goal of separating from others, and eventually a state of separation from the self.

For a *person* true freedom is choosing complete dependence on God who is completely free.

For an *individual*, true autonomy is choosing complete dependence on the self.

A *person* accepts the reality of God, other people and the physical world.

An *individual* rejects everything outside of the self as subjective, a non-reality (1995, p.28).

Clearly an *individual* therapist with a secular view is going to find it challenging to relate to a *person* who is seeking counseling and growth within a Christian context. The following is an examination of the actual counseling process in this light with respect to the five stages of counseling offered by Hackney and Cormier in *The Professional Counselor*.

Stage One — Rapport and Relationship Building

Hackney and Cormier state that "when the counselor establishes rapport with a client, the relationship includes such factors as respect, trust, and a sense of relative psychological comfort" (2001, p.24). Within a Christian context, finding common ground upon which to build rapport and trust in the therapeutic relationship requires that the therapist understand and honor the Christian perspective. As therapists, how can we enter into a "real relationship" with a client, unless we can appreciate the worldview held by that client? Colson stresses the importance of the worldview in the following quote:

> *Our choices are shaped by what we believe is real and true, right and wrong, good and beautiful. Our choices are shaped by our worldview. ... a person's worldview is intensely practical. It is simply the sum total of our beliefs about the world, the "big picture" that directs our daily decisions and actions. And understanding worldviews is extremely important (1999, p.13-14).*

Appreciating the *person's* worldview will lead to better empathic understanding, more effective questioning, and a greater capacity for effective goal setting. Empathic understanding will improve rapport and relationship building, when the counselor conveys such understanding with genuineness and respect for the client's beliefs and worldview, treating the client as a *person* rather than as an *individual*. This approach will provide an authentic sense of "psychological comfort" because it will allow the client to be at ease with his/her Christian identity. The end result is "good rapport" – something that Hackney and Cormier say "sets the stage for positive psychological growth, while poor rapport leads to undesirable or even counterproductive outcomes" (2001, p.25).

Stage Two — Assessment

This stage involves collecting and classifying information that helps to clarify the client's identity and his/her reasons for seeking counseling. Hackney and Cormier describe three aspects that are important in this stage:

> *First, assessment depends on the counselor's theoretical and philosophical view of human problems. Second, assessment depends on the conditions present in the client's situation and the counselor's understanding of those conditions. And third, assessment depends on the client's cultural frame of reference and the conditions that frame of reference imposes on the client's worldview (2001, p.27).*

Consequently, in addition to its significance in helping to establish rapport and build a therapeutic relationship, the concept of a clearly understandable worldview is essential to the assessment stage as well. The counselor needs to have an understanding of the beliefs and practices that guide the decisions and the actions of Christian *persons* in order to effectively assess and understand the client's situation.

Stage Three — Goal Setting

"The act of setting a goal involves making a commitment to a set of conditions, a course of action, or an outcome" (Hackney & Cormier, 2001). Later in the text the authors note that "within the multicultural counseling context, the effect of goal setting is less well understood by counselors" (2001, p. 107). Given the view of Samuel Huntingdon as stated in the beginning of this article, it is logical to view Christian counseling as an aspect of multicultural counseling, since religious and cultural traditions form our worldviews, and it is these worldviews that divide people more so than geographic boundaries. Hence, goal setting within a Christian context is less well understood by counselors. If Christians are attempting to discover what is true and live in step with *that* truth, while at the same time seeking counseling from a therapist who has been trained in self-psychology; there will be difficulties, conflicts, and misunderstandings because they fail to speak the same language.

An example may further illustrate this point. Several years ago a middle aged woman named Kathy came to see me for assistance with a problem she was experiencing at work. She was in upper management in a large organization which claimed to operate under the concepts offered by humanist psychology – a form of self-psychology. She found herself repeatedly in conflict because the humanist values in her work environment did not include God, yet they claimed to be founded on goodness. Her external world was in conflict with her core beliefs, and she was having difficulty resolving the conflict. In other words, her external world was treating people as *individuals*, while her internal world saw them as *persons*. Her job was to manage people in this conflicting environment. A secular counselor would never have been able to understand or appreciate Kathy's conflict. Christians are at odds with the world in many situations, and unless counselors can understand and appreciate the depth and the magnitude of their internal struggle, we will be unable to effectively help Christian clients meet their counseling needs.

Stage Four — Initiating Interventions

"The multicultural counselor uses the total spectrum of approaches *and* intervenes by understanding the client's cultural milieu and helping the client take charge of his/her life within that milieu" (2001, p.31). Once again the counselor is expected to understand the client's worldview in order to initiate appropriate interventions. The therapeutic plan that is developed and implemented reflects the results of the assessment process and the goals that were jointly established between client and therapist.

Throughout the therapeutic process there is dialogue between client and therapist. Useful guidelines for this dialogue come from an understanding of the Christian mind and an appreciation of how Christians think. In *The Christian Mind* Harry Blamires lists six marks of the Christian mind that may effectively contribute to this dialogue: supernatural orientation, awareness of evil, conception of the truth, acceptance of authority, concern for the person, and a sacramental view of life. It is good for Christian counselors to be aware of these marks of the Christian mind when dialoguing with clients.

Stage Five — Termination and Follow-up

Theoretically, counseling provides all types of clients with new ways of functioning and coping with life situations. Hopefully, through the course of Christian counseling, the client discovers what is true and begins to live in step with that truth. As confidence in the authentic self and dependence on God grow, the Christian client begins to recognize how to live effectively without the regular support of the therapist. Sessions get further apart and eventually cease, because the client has undertaken the process on his/her own and is now better able to recognize and live the truth with God's grace. Of course, traditional counseling would teach coping skills and new ways of functioning from a purely secular perspective, disregarding how the *person* is called by God. As part of the termination process in any counseling setting, there should be an understanding that further sessions may be necessary in the future, if there is a period of growth that requires assistance.

Summary of the Five Stages of Counseling

This five-stage process is often used by professional counselors, and it is an effective therapeutic process. However, the one missing link for Christians is the absence of a unified Christian approach to counseling – one which is based on Christian philosophy and modeled according to Christian thought, one which includes interventions that address the needs of the Christian population.

Hence, not only is there a need for counseling services to help the members of the Christian community, there is also a need for a unified approach to Christian counseling. This would allow Christians to seek counseling with greater comfort and peace of mind, because they would be more assured that the counsel being offered to them was based on a belief system that they embrace.

What is the Added Value of Christian Counseling?

Christian counseling addresses the whole person: their core beliefs and the way those beliefs are manifested in their lives through thoughts, attitudes, feelings, and behaviors. It allows people to deal with their issues in a context with which they are familiar, a context which supports their true identity. It provides a process through which they can grow in their authentic self and in their relationships with others and with God. Christian counseling supports and encourages Christians in their faith – a process that has positive effects on many aspects of mental and physical health and well-being. Christian counseling provides a process that Christians can feel comfortable using because they know that it does not contradict the beliefs and values of their faith. Christian counseling provides an environment in which we can establish goals and achieve outcomes that are meaningful because they are in line with our core beliefs – beliefs that support our true identity as children of God.

How Does Christian Counseling Relate to the Broader Field of Counseling?

As mentioned previously under the topic of goal setting, Christian counseling can be viewed as an aspect of multicultural counseling. Clearly, it does not meet the needs of all people and would not be applicable for those of a different faith. Freedom of religion applies to all people, and those of a different faith need to be counseled according to their beliefs.

Multicultural counseling offers a way to be culturally sensitive to people's needs. Since both religious and cultural traditions provide worldviews that serve to divide us, isn't it just as prudent to be "religiously sensitive" as it is to be "culturally sensitive?" Christian counseling is a branch of counseling that addresses the needs of Christians, just as Feminist Therapy addresses "women's issues" and Family Therapy addresses issues from a "systems perspective."

Christians need a form of therapy that addresses their unique needs, since those needs are often not met in traditional counseling. Instead, these needs are often unnoticed, rejected, suppressed, or denied in a traditional counseling setting. The result is needless suffering, because rather than being affirmed in their faith, Christians may be judged unfairly. Consequently, rather than providing healing, counselors might inflict more wounds. The following story is a case in point.

Ella's Story

People who have a strong faith and perhaps an unusual way of expressing it can be wrongfully diagnosed with the label "religious pre-occupation." Recently, while I was working in an inpatient mental health unit, I encountered a delightful elderly woman who was being evaluated for possible dementia with "religious pre-occupation." While standing in the hall with me one afternoon, Ella, a 91 year old African American woman, began to tell me her story. She told me how important her mother had been to her in her childhood years. She described her mother as being "filled with faith and very prayerful." Ella said that she had that reputation in the community. As Ella relayed the story to me she began to swell with pride and enthusiasm. She moved away from a conversational dialogue and entered a more charismatic way of speaking. As a Christian, I easily recognized this transition. (My initial insight about her charismatic roots was later confirmed when I took her psychosocial history. She told me of her baptism in a Pentecostal church.) The charismatic manner was simply part of the way she told her story. She was speaking with complete clarity, so I encouraged her to continue.

However, after a short time, she was interrupted by another patient on the unit who happened to overhear our conversation. The man who interrupted her had a strong need to feel that he was taking care of her. He proceeded to remind Ella of their conversation the previous day. He kept telling her to "stop that *keening*." Ella was confused by his words, and told him that she did not understand what he meant. He continued to refer to the previous conversation and some papers he had given to her. She agreed to look for them. He was not satisfied. He wanted confirmation that she understood him in that moment. Suddenly, a light went on for Ella, and she responded: "Oh, you mean words of human instruction. I see. You hold that above the word of Almighty God. I understand."

He never really heard what Ella said. He simply heard her say, "I understand." She became very meek and humble. She hugged him and thanked him kindly for his help. He went on his way and she continued her story.

Here was a woman who was being evaluated for dementia, and yet, she had clearer insight into the *real dynamics* of a conversation than someone that we would consider more mentally competent. She saw this man's judgment of her, knew that he had no capacity to understand her perspective, and humbly ended the conversation.

After he had gone, I smiled at Ella and nodded for her to continue. She continued speaking in the same charismatic tone, but in a softer voice. The outcome of our conversation was that she needed to share an internal struggle concerning the bitterness and regrets that she had accumulated because of the way she had lived her life. As she told her story, she expressed her contrition to God out loud. She would look back into her past and see some painful memory. Then she would express her feelings about it through her gestures and facial expressions. Afterward, she would ask God to forgive her, telling Him that she is trying to do better. She would declare, "I'm sorry, Lord. I'm *so* sorry, Lord!" After listening to her, I touched her arm gently, as I looked into her eyes and said firmly: "God knows that you are sorry, and He forgives you."

She immediately became peaceful. She let go of the charismatic speech and resumed her regular dialogue with me.

Shortly after this incident we all went to the psychotherapy group, where Ella shared with us another matter that was truly troubling her. She related to us how difficult the previous two months had been for her. She had lost two cousins and three neighbors. (Suddenly, the prospect of meeting God face to face had become very real to her. She needed to know that God loves her and forgives her sins. She wanted someone to tell her that her Christian beliefs are real.) *She* did not make this conscious connection. She simply knew how devastated she felt about losing so many people who were close to her in such a short period of time. (For me, a Catholic Christian, it impressed upon my mind how powerfully healing our sacrament of reconciliation can be.)

The group *listened* to her story. We *heard* what she had to say, and we gave her a sense of belonging. At the conclusion of the group session Ella remained in the room. She had a strong need to continue her conversation with us, as therapists. The group leader tried to get her to go to the next group. Ella had no interest in doing that. Finally, Ella reluctantly went into the hall. The door was closed for only a few seconds, when we heard knocking. It was Ella. She wanted to come back into the room. She said she was afraid to stand in the hall alone. Actually, she just wanted to be with us. She had not finished telling her story yet.

The group leader had another meeting outside the unit, and she also needed to complete a psychosocial history for Ella. I offered to do the psychosocial history. As Ella and I talked, she gave me several more opportunities to affirm her Christian faith. At one point she said, "We're all related somehow, aren't we?" I assured her that we are all brothers and sisters in Christ. She spoke of things in her past that caused her to feel anger and shame. Once again, she quietly told God how sorry she was and how she had tried to reform. I told her that we have a loving and forgiving God. Surely, if I, in my human weakness, could see her sorrow and pain, so could God. These words seemed to bring her comfort and allow her to let go of the pain and suffering that had been burdening her.

At the end of the interview, she thanked me for spending time with her, for listening to her story, and for affirming her faith. She knew that the interview was finished. She was at peace. She got up, allowed me to hug her, and went quietly back to her room.

The following day when I went to visit Ella, she immediately smiled and stood to greet me. Her mental faculties had begun to stabilize. She remembered me and our conversation from the previous day. The confusion from the delirium or pseudo-dementia had lifted, and she was recovering. How much of her recovery process was due to the affirmation of her Christian faith? We will never discover the answer to that question in this life!

Christians must be allowed to have a voice in their therapeutic process. Their beliefs need to be honored. They need to have coping skills that are consistent with their faith. If we can see the struggles of African Americans or Hispanics or women or victims of abuse, and allow them to have a voice in therapy, what prevents us from treating Christians with the same empathic understanding?

Writing this paper was an important part of my formation as a Christian counselor. It helped me to understand the need for Christian counseling on an intellectual level. More importantly, however, it provided a seed of inspiration in my mind. I had been using Christian based models in my healing and teaching for years. Perhaps God was calling me to provide the one missing link in Christian counseling – an approach based on Christian philosophy and modeled according to Christian thought. I accepted this seed of wisdom, and offered it up to God for His blessing. The seed germinated and grew during the months that it took me to complete my degree. The seed developed into the CompassionateCare Model, and it was presented as my final paper for graduation. Part III is dedicated to providing an understanding of that model.

Part III

CompassionateCare
from the Heart of Christ

Compassion has the power to heal and change lives.

Jesus cures the sick:
When he disembarked and saw the vast crowd,
his heart was moved with pity for them,
and he cured their sick. (Mt.14:14)

Jesus restores sight:
Moved with pity, Jesus touched their eyes.
Immediately they received their sight,
and followed him. (Mt. 20:34)

Jesus feeds the hungry:
Jesus summoned his disciples and said,
"My heart is moved with pity for the crowd,
for they have been with me for three days
and have nothing to eat.
I do not want to send them away hungry,
for fear they may collapse on the way. (Mt.15:32)

Jesus teaches the lost and ignorant:
When he disembarked and saw the vast crowd,
his heart was moved with pity for them,
for they were like sheep without a shepherd;
and he began to teach them many things. (Mk.6:34)

Jesus raises the dead:
As he drew near to the gate of the city,
a man who had died was being carried out,
the only son of his mother, and she was a widow.
A large crowd from the city was with her.
When the Lord saw her, he was moved with pity
for her and said to her, "Do not weep."
He stepped forward and touched the coffin;
at this the bearers halted, And he said,
"Young man, I tell you, arise!"
The dead man sat up and began to speak,
and Jesus gave him to his mother. (Lk 7:12-15)

Compassion

Compassion walks the city street
And listens for uncertain feet
That seek a home they cannot find
Because the heart that leads is blind.
Compassion holds a steady light
To show the way through chill of night
And takes the homeless by the hand
To lead them to a warmer land.

Compassion walks where life is hard,
Where eyes are blank and faces marred
By pain too great to understand,
And shoulders those too weak to stand.
Compassion is the Shepherd's name:
Who from the halls of heaven came
To travel landscapes bare and bleak
For those that only love would seek.

Compassion does not tire or sleep
But walks wherever sufferers weep
Through ages past and still to come,
Until the world is gathered home
To rest at last where mercy reigns
and heals all ill and stills all pains.
And there Compassion's walk will cease,
Where God is all, and all is peace.

13

CompassionateCare
A Christian Model of Wellness

Your love is before my eyes,
I walk guided by your faithfulness. (Ps. 26:3)

The CompassionateCare Model emerged as I studied the writings of Conrad Baars, a Christian psychiatrist. He referred to himself as a true Christian, not a secular humanist. In *Feeling and Healing Your Emotions* Baars states: "I write about the meaning of man's emotional life as an integral, well-defined part of his God-given nature." Baars discusses *truths about the emotions*, providing information that validates the experience of human emotion. His writing encourages people to honor human emotions as psychic motors that produce motion and energy to make our lives easier. Rather than seeing emotions as a troublesome part of human nature that needs to be suppressed or disguised, Baars presents emotions as the fundamental tools that move us forward on our life's journey.

In addition to his discussion about the emotional aspect of the person, Baars describes the higher faculty of the intellect as having two distinct parts: the Reasoning Mind and the Intuitive Mind. The Reasoning Mind is the "working mind." It is used to *think things through*, providing analysis, judgment, reason, or abstraction. The Reasoning Mind is subordinate to the superior aspect of the intellect, the Intuitive Mind. Through the Intuitive Mind we *perceive truths directly* through our appreciation of nature, art, and music. The Intuitive Mind is especially active during prayer and meditation, when we can communicate directly with God through the Holy Spirit. Baars was convinced that the information presented in *Feeling and Healing Your Emotions* would "deepen the reader's belief in the healing power of the Holy Spirit, as well as his understanding of how the Spirit works with and for human beings."

Baars includes a commentary on the will as a final component of the "human hierarchy that guides movement." He describes the will as the *prime mover*. The will moves us to act by allowing choices that either: abide by reason, ignore reason, or go against reason. As the *prime mover*, the will is guided by the integrated functioning of the emotions, the Reasoning Mind, and the Intuitive Mind. The will governs the process of decision making and appropriate action by "respectfully listening to the emotions" and "striving for the good" together with the emotional aspect. The will is moved by reason that teaches us what is *truly good,* **and** by the emotion of *desire for that good*.

In an effort to digest and assimilate Baars concept of the "human hierarchy that guides movement," I created the charts that appear on the following two pages. A greater understanding of the process is facilitated by first reviewing the *truths about the emotions*. Baars discusses these truths throughout the book. I found it useful to gather them together as the cornerstone of the hierarchy. A meditative review of these truths has the power to transform the way we think about the *gift* of human emotion. After thoughtful consideration of these truths, the reader may examine "The Human Hierarchy that Guides Movement" by starting from the bottom with the **emotions** and moving up toward the **will** at the top. This reinforces an understanding of the natural flow of the process.

Truths about the Emotions

- *All our emotions, in their "pure" state, are good and necessary for healthy living.*

- *There are no negative or "bad" emotions.*

- *Emotions are natural tools with specific functions.*

- *All emotions have a need to be guided by reason and to be allowed to make their particular contribution to healthy living.*

- *Any effort to interfere with the natural function of emotions will have adverse repercussions.*

- *Every emotion is accompanied by certain physiological changes, which must also be recognized and allowed to be.*

- *All emotions must be allowed to grow to full capacity and become integrated with and subordinate to reason and will.*

- *Emotions must be cultured, educated and refined, so that they will respond readily to the will informed by reason.*

- *It is **not** true that every emotion must be expressed or gratified (beyond the naturally occurring physical changes which are part of all emotions).*

- *It is **not** the task of the emotions to interfere with one another or to control each other. They all operate on the same level.*

The Human Hierarchy
That Guides Movement
(Begin at the bottom of the page and read to the top.)

THE WILL
The Prime Mover

Moves us to action by allowing choices that either:
1. Abide by reason; **2.** Ignore reason; **3.** Go against reason

*It rules democratically by respectfully listening to the emotions **and** striving for the good together with them.*
*It is moved by reason that shows us what is truly good, **and** by the emotion of desire for that good.*

THE MIND
The Higher Faculty of the Intellect

Intuitive Mind	Reasoning Mind
Superior	*Subordinate*
Directly perceives truths (independent of any reasoning process) via the arts, nature and directly from God through the Spirit.	Working or discursive mind. Determines which courses of action are proper under the circumstances – using analysis, reason, judgment or abstraction.

THE EMOTIONS
Psychic Motors that produce Motion and Energy to make our lives easier

---

Humane Emotions	Utilitarian Emotions
"Pleasure appetite"	*"Utility appetite"*
(Cause us to be moved)	(Cause us to move, act, do)
Love	Fear
Desire	Courage
Joy	Despair
Hate	Hope
Aversion	Anger
Sadness	

I found Baars discussion of these four integral aspects – the emotions, the reasoning mind, the intuitive mind, and the will – of the human person to be fascinating. Reflecting on Baars concept of these parts as components of our "God-given nature," I began to think about each one as an independent *gift*, presenting each aspect to God and asking for His blessing. God allowed me to gain experiential understanding of each aspect by entering into the description provided by Conrad Baars. Fueled by an attitude of wonder and awe, I began to see a model emerge in my mind – a model that comes to life as it is considered in light of the process of human development. The model is called CompassionateCare because it was revealed to me through my devotion to the Sacred Heart of Jesus.

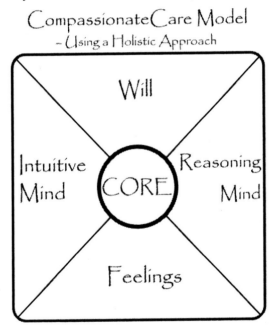

This Therapeutic Model is based on a theory presented by Conrad Baars in *Feeling and Healing Your Emotions*.

The Significance of the Therapeutic Model

The Emotions

Healthy emotions provide a constant source of energy that moves us forward in life. They are a source of growth, learning, and healing, when they are recognized and freely expressed in a healthy way. When they are suppressed, excessively controlled, or unacknowledged, we are robbed of their necessary contribution to a whole and healthy lifestyle. Emotions need to develop so they can be *integrated with* and allowed to become *subordinate to* reason and will.

Part of our work as therapists is to help clients recognize, accept, understand, and effectively use their emotions in making decisions and taking action on them. Emotions must be cultured, educated, and refined to allow them to respond readily to the will informed by reason.

Historically, the emotions have been seen as enemies of our higher faculties and the spirit. A common belief is that the human will must be trained to act *against* the emotions in order to lead a virtuous life. This is a fear-based belief that attempts to protect us from impulsive behavior. Society has been further influenced by the teaching of Immanuel Kant, who considered all human feelings to be pathological (Baars, 1970).

These erroneous beliefs have influenced the lives of families and individuals, causing them to judge emotions and make efforts to interfere with their natural function. Efforts to interfere with the natural operation of human emotion result in adverse repercussions, perhaps in the form of anxiety or depression or some other disorder.

As therapists we need to validate the importance of the client's feelings, as well as the physiological changes that accompany them. Feelings that have been suppressed need to be allowed to emerge. Then clients need to be taught how to manage them through the proper use of the mind and the will. By being comfortable with our own feelings and relating to our clients from our feeling center, we can teach clients that feelings are good and necessary for healthy living. In addition to this indirect manner of addressing feelings, we can cognitively educate clients about the interactive process among the feelings, the intuitive mind, the reasoning mind, and the will.

The Reasoning Mind

Often the reasoning mind is an area of considerably more comfort than the realm of the emotions. Many people have learned to escape from the pain of their emotions to the relative safety of the reasoning mind where they can intellectualize their pain, rationalize their poor choices, and justify their inappropriate behaviors. Often, clients find themselves in therapy because they need help to achieve greater health in the functioning of their reasoning mind.

Many people have not developed the skill to effectively *think things through.* Sometimes people temporarily lose sight of that ability due to stressful situations. In addition, many of us have incorporated irrational beliefs into our thought patterns, and we need help to learn healthier ways of thinking.

The reasoning mind is a great asset, when we develop the skill to use it properly for analysis, critical thinking, judgment, or abstract reasoning. The working mind helps us consider feedback from the emotions and the intuitive mind to determine which courses of action are appropriate under the circumstances.

As therapists we have the opportunity and the challenge to assess the function of the reasoning mind with our clients as they reveal their history and presenting problems to us. In the course of this dialogue we can note deficits and opportunities for improved functioning. These ideas can then be incorporated into our treatment plans.

The Intuitive Mind

For many individuals the intuitive mind is not as familiar as the reasoning mind. Often people view intuition as a special gift, available to a select few. In fact, each individual is gifted with an intuitive mind that is paired with the reasoning mind. As a team they work together to guide the higher faculty of the intellect. It is probably surprising for most people to learn that the intuitive mind is, in fact, the superior of the two aspects of the intellect, while the reasoning mind is the subordinate aspect. What a shame that so many individuals feel out-of-touch with the superior aspect of their intellect!

The intuitive mind is superior in that it *directly perceives truths* independent of any reasoning process. The intuitive mind is enlivened by appreciating the elements of nature, art, or music. Embracing the fundamental beliefs of one's faith and finding union with God through prayer and meditation also activate the intuitive mind, helping people grow in the Spirit. Thus, the intuitive mind offers us an indirect connection to God through nature and other aspects of created beauty, as well as a direct connection through our faith. The intuitive mind is where we can identify and validate our spiritual aspect and contemplate the truths of our faith.

Through contemplation and reflection the intuitive mind

allows us to receive insight and wisdom that is beyond the working of the reasoning mind. As therapists we can use that insight and wisdom to guide the therapeutic process. It helps us with assessment and goal setting, as well as providing us with guidance for various interventions. In addition to being useful for the therapist, knowledge of the intuitive mind can be imparted directly to our clients. They can be taught to acknowledge their own intuition and cultivate the insight that is available from this superior aspect of the intellect.

The Will

It is the will that ultimately moves us to act. Under ideal circumstances the will rules democratically by respectfully listening to the emotions and striving for the good together with them. In this striving for good, the will is moved by reason that shows us what is truly good, and by the emotion of desire for that good. Ultimately, however, the will is free to choose to abide by reason, ignore reason or go against reason. The will is influenced by our biases, our wounds, our fears, our poor patterns, and our selfishness, as well as by our desire for good.

When strongly influenced by our unhealthy emotions, the will governs our behavior and leads to *acting out*. When strongly influenced by the imbalance between the mind and the emotions in which the mind attempts to control or contain the emotions, the will governs our behavior through the defense mechanisms of rationalization, intellectualization, denial, isolation of affect, or suppression.

As we accept the emotions and learn to manage them in a more proper balance with the healthy influence of both the intuitive mind and the reasoning mind, the will is given greater freedom to make healthy choices. Consequently, proper therapeutic attention to the health of the emotions and the two aspects of the intellect will help clients achieve greater freedom of choice, and result in healthier choices.

The above discussion of the CompassionateCare Model provides only a structure and a simple understanding of the component parts of the model. Greater appreciation of the model is achieved by examining the function of the component parts both individually and as a whole. The following chapters demonstrate how the model can be used therapeutically to facilitate an understanding of the process of human and spiritual development, and provide healing of developmental wounds that may have been sustained. The information presented can also provide insight to parents, teachers, and other individuals who are responsible for the formation of children.

14

The CompassionateCare Model: Focus on Feelings and the Will

*Let your "Yes" mean "Yes,"
and your "No" mean "No." (Mt. 5:37)*

A thorough understanding of the CompassionateCare Model begins with the section on feelings. Developmentally, feelings are the first of the four gifts to emerge. As children we are predominantly *feeling beings* until the age of six or seven years old. Through the developmental wisdom of God we are given those years to experience and learn to use the gift of feelings – both body sensations and emotions. Through sensory awareness and sensory appetite children begin to experience impulses. The gift of curiosity leads to exploration of one's own body, as well as one's surroundings. This natural developmental progression leads to sitting, standing, walking, and so on.

By responding to internal impulses the child progresses through various developmental stages. Curiosity provides the desire to move, and exploration is the activity through which sensory knowledge is acquired. Young children have no understanding of what is safe or unsafe. It is the responsibility of adults to provide guidance in these matters. As curiosity propels the child into exploration, it is the responsibility of adults to prevent children from harm by saying "No." This is the first opportunity we have to teach our children about the meaning of the word "No." It is also the first opportunity our children have to resist or rebel. Children learn very quickly whether or not our "No" means "No." They are experts at testing boundaries. A "No" that is non-existent, wishy-washy, apprehensive, or confused gives a child permission to proceed as they choose. Clearly, children are not mature enough to make good choices. They require the guidance of a caring adult who is courageous enough to provide proper discipline, as well as unconditional love.

The responsibility God has given us to impart effective guidance to our children cannot be underestimated. Learning to say "No" and mean "No" offers critical developmental guidance to children. Children who fail to receive such guidance fail to develop self-control and a sense of internal discipline. They develop impulsive and/or aggressive behavior, and they may find themselves on a path toward a personality disorder.

This concept became clearer in my understanding as I counseled a young girl regarding her aggressive behavior. Her behavior was so out of control that she was disruptive at school, at home, and in extracurricular activities. By the age of eight she had already become very difficult to reach. I prayed extensively for guidance in handling her situation. She was the child of a drug-addicted mother, and she was currently living under the care of another family member. Although frustrated and at wits end, this other family member truly loved the child and wanted to help her.

In an effort to explain the dynamics of the situation to the caregiver, I was inspired to use the newly emerging CompassionCare Model. During a counseling session I drew a picture of the model on a piece of paper. I explained that children are *feeling beings* who have impulses to act, and that their actions must be tempered by adult guidance. This guidance requires adults to say "No" and mean

Chapter Fourteen

"No." If adults fail in their responsibility, children learn to act on impulse. This creates a pattern of behavior that causes the will to be driven solely by the feelings. The feeling aspect never has an opportunity to develop self-control or internal discipline. As a result, the child experiences a feeling and takes that feeling into action immediately.

It was as if I watched a light go on inside the caregiver's head. She immediately responded: "That is exactly what happened to Karen. Her mother never told her 'No.' She let the children do anything they wanted to do. Now she (Karen) thinks she should have anything she wants, anytime she wants it. That picture tells her story."

For people like Karen it is as if the reasoning mind and the intuitive mind fail to participate in the decision making process. Actions are determined exclusively by feelings. This dysfunctional use of the human will plagues adults as well as children. Sarah is a case in point. She was a long term client and divorced mother of several children. I often described her as moving from crisis to crisis. The interventions I used to correct this behavior had only a minimal effect. One day, years after our sessions had ceased, I was called to her home to use holistic healing methods in an effort to ease the severe pain she was suffering from a scooter accident. She was brush burned from head to toe. During her treatment in the emergency room the staff had called her children to her bedside, fearing that she was near death.

When I arrived at her home, she was lying on the couch unable to move because she was in so much pain. Gently, I began to treat the wounds and reduce her inflammation. Struggling to speak, she told me about the accident. On an impulse, she went out and bought a scooter. Without reading the instruction manual or taking any lessons, she

141

decided to go for a ride. The scooter went out of control and Sarah's body was dragged across a parking lot. When the EMTs arrived on the scene, they expressed little hope for her condition. Sarah finished her story with tears in her eyes, telling me how frightening it was to have her children called to the hospital because she was near death.

At the time, I was just starting to use the CompassionateCare Model in my work. It immediately came to mind as Sarah related her story to me. She had a long-standing pattern of acting on impulse. This behavior caused her to live her life moving from crisis to crisis. Even though Sarah was weak and in pain, I felt a strong urge to describe the CompassionateCare Model to her. Through God's grace she was able to hear my words and understand what I was trying to tell her. I saw the *light of knowing* in her eyes. She was finally able to understand her own behavior. I began to realize the powerful insight that can be imparted to people through the CompassionateCare Model.

For both Karen and Sarah, I used a modified version of the CompassionateCare Model to emphasize the strong connection between feelings and action. This version is depicted on the following page. Both the reasoning mind and the intuitive mind are shadowed in this version in order to emphasize their lack of influence in making decisions and implementing them.

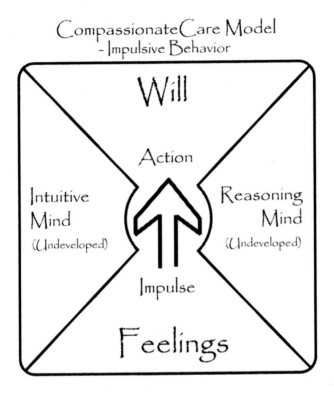

CompassionateCare Model
- Impulsive Behavior

Will

Action

Intuitive Mind
(Undeveloped)

Reasoning Mind
(Undeveloped)

Impulse

Feelings

The *Impulsive Behavior* model demonstrates the fluid connection between the feelings and the will to act, when the feelings operate without self-control and without the influence of the reasoning mind or the intuitive mind. This represents the dysfunction that occurs when "No" has not been properly used or understood. "No" that means "No" creates an obstacle between the feelings and the will, preventing impulsive behavior. The CompassionateCare Model can be used to demonstrate this change as shown in the model for Learning Self-Control .

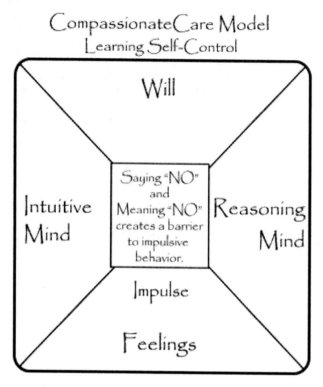

CompassionateCare Model
Learning Self-Control

Will

Intuitive Mind

Saying "NO" and Meaning "NO" creates a barrier to impulsive behavior.

Reasoning Mind

Impulse

Feelings

The model for ***Learning Self-Control*** creates the belief: "You can't always get what you want." It teaches self-control and initiates internally imposed discipline. This is an essential step in developing healthy adult behavior and in establishing the important Christian characteristic of self-denial.

When "No" is used as an obstacle, it creates opportunities for us to choose a different path. During childhood years it can teach patience, when we have to wait for our desire to become a reality. It may open the intuitive mind by prompting us to imagine what it would be like, *if* we could have what we want. It can also teach us that the reality of life is that sometimes the answer is simply "No."

In later years, after the intellect has had an opportunity to develop, "No" can prompt the reasoning mind to find alternative paths through analysis or critical thinking. Or it can prompt the intuitive mind to seek alternatives through insight and inspiration.

When "No" is presented as an obstacle, it provides an opportunity to learn healthy coping behavior. "No" is a form of rejection. It can create a sense of disappointment. Disappointment does *not feel good,* **and** it is a reality of life. Disappointment also has many lessons:

- It can teach us to accept reality.
- It can teach us patience.
- It can teach us perseverance.
- It can teach us detachment.
- It can teach us self-denial.

If everything in life "goes our way," we miss opportunities to grow in Christian virtue by learning acceptance, patience, perseverance, detachment, and self-denial. Perhaps disappointment is a gift from God!

In an effort to further understand the *gift* of disappointment in light of the CompassionateCare Model, I offered it up to God and asked for His blessing. He responded with a series of images to expand my understanding. In the first image God rotated the CompassionateCare Model by a ¼ turn and made it in the image of a bulldozer. I saw myself driving the bulldozer with the will positioned directly in front of me, receiving the full support of the feeling aspect, the reasoning mind, and the intuitive mind. I was moving straight along the path, when suddenly an obstacle appeared, covering the entire path. From the perspective of my *physical vision* that was **all** I could see.

However, through the *gift of supernatural vision* I could see DANGER ahead on my path, and I could see the hand of God guiding me along a newly created path that veered to the right, leading away from the dangerous area ahead. This vision showed me that rather than being disappointed about an obstacle in my path, I needed to be grateful to God for redirecting me before I made a mistake. This action made by God *as my Father* is the same type of action we are called to make as parents, protecting our children from things that might be harmful to them. Sometimes our children can be so strong willed that redirecting them can feel like an encounter with a bulldozer!

For those of you who understand concepts better when they are presented in concrete forms, like pictures, an image of this vision is given in the diagram shown below. It is the first level in a developmental progression that moves

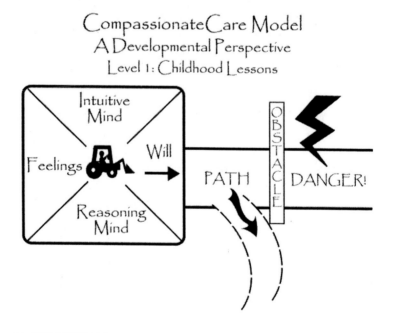

from childhood lessons, through mature human development and culminates in authentic human spirituality.

The Level 1 diagram demonstrates the first stage of the CompassionateCare Model when it is viewed from a developmental perspective. It reveals the importance of having external factors that create obstacles on our path, preventing us from entering areas of danger. This is the model used by adults to impose guidance and proper formation on children.

The Level 2 diagram that follows demonstrates a later developmental stage during which we learn to recognize the obstacles and dangers on our own. I had to mystically *enter into* the model in order to understand God's message.

As I imagined myself in the feeling section of the Level 2 image there was an urge to move and take action. I felt that this urge was stifled by the reasoning mind. As my conscious awareness moved into the reasoning mind, I realized that it contained a STOP sign because it recognized the obstacle that was presented on my path. Recognizing this need to STOP caused my feeling center to initially experience disappointment, frustration, and perhaps anger. However, my intuitive mind came to the rescue, calling me to pray for acceptance, patience, strength, wisdom, and discernment. This experience summarizes the internal struggle that often occurs when we encounter obstacles and attempt to deal with the frustration that follows. The Level 2 image appears on the following page.

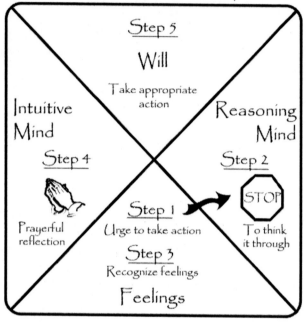

CompassionateCare Model
A Developmental Perspective
Level 2: Mature Human Development

A third developmental image appeared. It demonstrated an additional level of development. This image was one of a growing plant that had been pruned. It defined a more spiritual application of the CompassionateCare Model based on the words of Jesus in the Gospel of John:

> *I am the true vine, and my Father is the vine grower. He takes away every branch in me that does not bear fruit, and everyone that does he prunes so that it bears more fruit. (Jn. 15:1-2)*

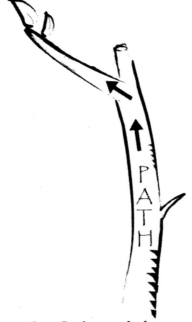

CompassionateCare Model
A Developmental Perspective
Level 3: Authentic Human Spirituality

In the image that God revealed to me, the branch that had been pruned was growing a lead shoot. It was prevented from growing straight along its current path, and instead, it branched into greater fullness for the plant because it had been pruned. Obstacles have the same effect on people that pruning has on plants (See the image depicting Level 3).

Therefore, if God wants us to grow in greater fullness as His children, He will provide obstacles on our path. These obstacles facilitate our developmental journey from Level 1: *Childhood Lessons* through Level 2: *Mature Human Development* and into Level 3: *Authentic Human Spiritual-*

ity. The human reality is that we can't always get what we want, AND that is a *good thing* because it teaches us to continually recognize that our mission is to seek and do the will of God.

Many times discovering God's will for us develops through a course of trial and error. The lesson we need to learn is to acknowledge the human emotions that are associated with meeting obstacles and encountering rejection. By learning to properly use these emotions, we are guided through the developmental process that was outlined in the above series of images. As these emotions are acknowledged they should be offered to God through a humble and contrite heart, asking for acceptance, patience, strength, discernment, and wisdom. In addition, we need to express gratitude for the obstacle because it is probably a gift from God. The reasoning mind that helps us to recognize the obstacle and STOP moving in that direction is also a gift. This reasoning goes against human logic because it is the wisdom of God whose thoughts and ways are far above the thoughts and ways provided by mere human wisdom. We come to know these thoughts and ways by using the intuitive mind to reflect on our faith. In this way we transcend mere human wisdom and discover the wisdom of God.

> *Indeed, though one be perfect among the sons of men, if Wisdom, who comes from You, be not with him, he shall be held in no esteem...Send her forth from Your holy heavens and from Your glorious throne dispatch her. That she may be with me and work with me, that I may know what is Your pleasure. For she knows and understands all things, and will guide me discreetly in my affairs and safeguard me in her glory; ...For what man knows God's counsel,*

*or who can conceive what the Lord intends? ... Or
who ever knew Your counsel, except You had given
Wisdom and sent Your Holy Spirit from on high?
And thus were the paths of those on earth made
straight, and men learned what was Your pleasure,
and were saved by Wisdom. (Wis. 9: 6, 10-11,13,
17-18)*

Wisdom is acquired through human experience that is
honored as a gift from God and offered to Him through
meditation and reflection on life events. Obstacles provide
the opportunity to pause and reflect. They have the power
to teach us about the will of God. We first learn to experience this process as children, when we are told "No" by
those who mean "No." Only when our "No" means "No"
can our "Yes" truly mean "Yes."

In my education as a healer we were instructed to participate in a very simple exercise. In groups of two we
were told to make a request of our partner: "May I touch
you?" The person hearing the request was told to respond
"Yes" sometimes and "No" at other times. The request
was made several times. The person who made the request was instructed to focus on how they felt when they
heard "No." Regardless of how kindly the word "No"
was spoken, there was a sense of rejection inside each one
of us every time we heard "No."

This was an important lesson. Just as important was the
understanding that when people are able to respond "No,"
you can trust that their "Yes" truly means "Yes." I encourage the reader to try this little exercise with a partner
and experience the power of this understanding.

15

The CompassionateCare Model: Focus on the Intellect and the Will

If then you were raised with Christ,
seek what is above,
where Christ is seated at the right hand of God.
Think of what is above, not of what is on earth.
For you have died and your life is hidden
with Christ in God. (Col. 3: 1-3)

Before we can come to the mature spiritual understanding presented in the above scripture passage, we must first experience the stages of human development that cultivate the *self.* If we are called to die to self, we must first know who that self is. We must engage in the process of human development.

The gift of our human experience begins with feelings and impulses as we discussed in the previous chapter. Through our feeling center we begin to branch out and enter the higher faculty of the intellect, including the reasoning mind and the intuitive mind. We are prepared to enter both aspects of the intellect by the way we engage in life experiences through our feelings. Feelings can be affirming and validating. Feelings can also be confusing and unsettling. Learning to manage the strong urges produced by our feelings is a challenging task for children, especially when they do not understand the reasoning behind the choices that are imposed on them by adults.

How often do small children ask "Why," when they are given instructions? When my children were young, I spent countless hours trying to help them understand "why." Because children have only the capacity for concrete thought, they must be instructed in ways that allow them to see and touch what is being presented. Once they make the mental connection, their minds can expand to understand new concepts.

Often I would use stories to help Lauren understand difficult concepts. It was a process that I had developed over the years without being consciously aware of what I was doing. One day Lauren asked me to explain a concept that was far beyond her ability to comprehend. I explained that she was too young to understand. She immediately responded: "Then tell me the story about it, Mom." I suddenly realized that I had established a pattern of story telling to help her understand. I also realized that Jesus used story telling as a primary means of explaining things that are beyond our human comprehension. By following the feelings through the story line, children begin to achieve intellectual understanding and develop a process for *thinking things through*.

During the past two years I have had the privilege of designing and implementing a Wellness Program for the Altoona Central Catholic Schools. My desire was to teach them about the various aspects of the CompassionateCare Model and impart experiential understanding that would serve them well throughout their lives.

In addition to teaching them about feelings, thoughts, and behaviors; I developed a series of programs to teach them "life skills," such as problem solving, communication, and conflict resolution. It was a challenge to provide these lessons to students from kindergarten through fifth grade. Although they are all technically in the stage of concrete operations as far as their mental development is concerned, they are at very different levels of ability. While third, fourth, and fifth grade students easily acquired an understanding of the concepts through role playing and other interactive exercises; the younger children were not yet ready to participate in these activities.

In order to help them understand the concept of problem solving, I used a problem I had experienced and "told them the story about it" so they could work through the process of problem solving with me. Briefly, the problem I had involved my desire to build a grotto to honor Our Lady of Perpetual Help at our retreat center. During the two years that I tried to build the grotto, it rained and rained and rained. The ground never had a chance to dry.

In addition to the constant rain, the location selected for the grotto was at the bottom of the mountain (beside the chapel) where it collected all the rainfall from above. The problem was not only the rainfall and the runoff. There were natural springs on our property above the area where the grotto was planned, as well as a large lake on a neighboring property. These sources of water created even more water flow into the grotto area.

To help the children understand the problem, I created a model of the side of the mountain, and I took pictures of the runoff, the springs, and the lake. I included the pictures in a book that told the story of my problem and how I solved it. As I read the story to the children, I paused and let them gather around the model to see what I was explaining. This was the first lesson I presented during the school year. Those children could still recall the problem and the solution at the end of the year without any review of the concept. Because of the teaching method they were able to integrate what they had learned, and the knowledge was assimilated in a way that allowed them to recall it.

The concepts of communication and conflict resolution may seem to be too complicated for young minds to understand. However, when the children were given a basic definition of the words and taught about the concepts through a story, they were easily able to understand. I told them that communication was all about speaking clearly and listening carefully. In order to impress upon them how easy it is to develop *mis*communication, we played the "Telephone Game." I started a message around the circle and waited until the message returned to me. Then we compared the beginning message with the ending message. They were quite different. To further impress upon the children the importance of communication, I showed them a cartoon version of the story of Helen Keller. By watching the movie they were able to understand the importance of communication because they could see how difficult life would be without it.

We went through a similar process to understand conflict resolution. We talked about being selfish versus being generous, and lying versus telling the truth. Then I explained how people fight sometimes because someone is being selfish or someone is lying. When these fights occur, they tear people apart. That is called conflict. Bringing people back together is called resolution. Sometimes we need other people to bring us back together after we fight. I gave the older children a process to follow for conflict resolution, and I let them role play. Two children were in conflict and one child was the mediator. They actually worked through some real life issues in their role play. The younger children were not yet able to engage in a role play exercise. Instead, they watched a cartoon version about the story of Solomon – a king whose wisdom made him an expert in conflict resolution.

This same style of teaching works with difficult concepts in anatomy and physiology. Last year I designed a relay game for the children to play so they could understand the functioning of the senses, the nervous system, and the brain. When I wanted to teach them about nutrition, I had them *create* foods by using Lego blocks. We used different colored blocks to represent carbohydrates, proteins, and fats. Half of the class built the foods on Lego boards, while the other half of the class became parts of the digestive system. Then we fed the "food" to the "digestive system," and watched how the *building blocks of the food* became the *building blocks of the body*.

Because of the God-given gift of curiosity – the desire to know – children seek understanding. If a path for understanding is presented in a way that allows them to engage that knowledge through concrete operations, they learn new concepts and critical thinking skills. If the learning experience is *fun*, it stimulates their natural thirst for knowledge. Learning new concepts and developing the ability to *think things through* establishes a sense of competence and mastery, leading to positive growth in self-esteem.

When learning *feels good*, children want to continue doing it, and learning becomes a lifelong endeavor. Over time children move beyond the stage of concrete operations and into abstract reasoning. Then they no longer need *relay games* to teach them about the brain or *building blocks* to teach them about food and the process of digestion. They develop the ability to assimilate this knowledge as they read about these different concepts. This is the natural process of development for the reasoning mind as it learns to use the gift of human understanding.

Of course, this is what happens in a perfect world. In the real world children are exposed to human weaknesses that manifest in the form of ignorance, manipulation, lies, attempts to control, erroneous thinking, oppression, and so on. These experiences create distortions in our thought processes.

As adults we are then saddled with the responsibility of sorting these things out, and finding the truth about ourselves and the world around us. The only effective way I have discovered for finding and living the truth is by "putting on the mind of Christ."

Human weaknesses cause us to develop a false self as a form of protection. That false self must be removed in order for us to discover the true self. Removal of the false self is a process that occurs throughout our lives as we discover our own wounds and weaknesses that are in need of healing.

As we heal we are *"strengthened with power through His Spirit in the inner self" (Eph. 3:16)*, and *"although our outer self (false self) is wasting away, our inner self (true self) is being renewed day by day" (II Cor. 4:16)*. In this way *"He will change our lowly body to conform with His glorified body by the power that enables Him also to bring all things into subjection to Himself" (Phil. 3:20)*.

By circling through the right side of the CompassionateCare Model (see the image on page 160), moving from feelings, through the reasoning mind and into the will, we develop the gift of reason. We learn to use the positive qualities of the self to exert healthy self-control and establish a method for taking appropriate action by *thinking things through*. A healthy reasoning mind allows us to plan and organize. It allows us to use the scientific method to determine what is right and true. It helps us go through a process of trial and error, learning to eliminate certain things, while retaining others. The reasoning mind allows us to develop the critical thinking skills that are necessary for the proper functioning of the will.

However, the reasoning mind does not work alone to influence the will. The reasoning mind sorts and processes feelings, presenting them to the will through the gift of self-control. This is an important part of the functioning of the will; however, it is only half of the process that exists in a well-balanced state. While the right side of the CompassionateCare Model teaches us a structured way to work through a decision making process, the left side of the model provides the freedom to acquire infused knowledge from outside the self. The right side of the model helps us gain a sense of mastery over life events, and the left side of the model helps us enter an "allowing state" through which we can receive inspiration and insight through the power of the Holy Spirit. These two complementary pathways work together to influence the proper functioning of the will. Both processes are depicted in the Well-Balanced State diagram shown on the following page.

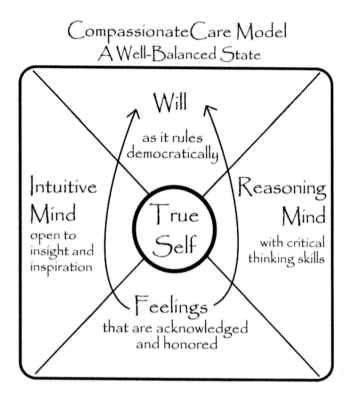

CompassionateCare Model
A Well-Balanced State

Will
as it rules
democratically

Intuitive
Mind
open to
insight and
inspiration

True
Self

Reasoning
Mind
with critical
thinking skills

Feelings
that are acknowledged
and honored

Just as we need to proceed through a developmental process to form the reasoning mind, we also need to undergo a developmental process to allow the intuitive mind to open and mature. We begin this journey in childhood through our ability to use the imagination. Children often create imaginary friends and fictional places – where they escape in their minds. They play games, pretending to be different characters who experience a variety of events. All of this "playing" through imagination prepares the intuitive mind to open and begin to taste the reality of mystery and embrace the realm of the supernatural.

When children are told "No," they have the option to *create in their minds* what they wanted to experience. In this way they can develop the capacity to dream and envision. Some children are born with a great capacity to envision. In the book of Genesis Joseph, son of Israel, was described by his brothers as a "master dreamer." He had a supernatural gift that allowed him to see things that others failed to see. This gift of vision can be acknowledged and encouraged to develop, or it can be suppressed. It can also develop in unhealthy ways, when people get caught up in fantasy or *magical thinking* as a means of escaping reality.

When the developmental process proceeds in a healthy way, we develop the capacity to dream or envision, and we use that vision to form a realistic goal that we can achieve. Ideally, from a Christian perspective that goal would be formulated according to the will and plan of God, and implemented by His grace in conjunction with our human efforts. This is how creative and innovative people bring new things into being.

Another healthy means of using the creativity of the intuitive mind is by developing the ability to appreciate beauty and reflect on God's goodness. Through meditation we access the intuitive mind, opening doors to the divine and welcoming the power of God's Spirit. This allows us to see our lives in relation to the mysteries of the life of Christ. It promotes growth in piety and wisdom because we find access to the thoughts and ways of God.

A healthy intuitive mind responds to the challenge of obstacles on our path by creating new and different alternatives that far exceed the goals of the original plan. When this capacity to envision is harnessed and united to a well-functioning reasoning mind, the two work together to accomplish great things through the proper functioning of the will.

Through this dual process I was able to create and implement the lesson plans for the Wellness Program that I designed for the Altoona Central Catholic Schools. Both the intuitive mind and the reasoning mind were actively engaged throughout the writing of this book. It was only through the coordinated efforts of the intuitive mind and the reasoning mind, as they were influenced by strong feelings of desire, that allowed me to conceive and build a 62-acre retreat center to serve the people of God.

My commitment to know, love, and serve God has enabled me to grow in holiness and experience a greater fullness of life. Because I allowed Christ to dwell in my heart through faith, I became rooted and grounded in love. Through Him I discovered the strength to comprehend the love of God that surpasses knowledge. This love created a fullness within me that bears fruit in abundance because I practice living in a Well-Balanced State, fully acknowledging and using my emotions, my reasoning mind, my intuitive mind, my will as it is guided by the will of God.

16

The CompassionateCare Model: Summary Descriptions

*For creation awaits with eager expectation
the revelation of the children of God;
For creation was made subject to futility,
not of its own accord but because of the one who
subjected it, in hope that creation itself would be set free
from slavery to corruption and share in the glorious
freedom of the children of God. (Rom. 8: 19-21)*

We are set free through the cross of Christ. By His wounds we are healed. We are healed of the brokenness that manifests itself in unhealthy behaviors. We are restored to physical wholeness, and we are elevated to spiritual wholeness through reconciliation to God in Christ.

In our **Physical Brokenness** our thoughts and ways are far from the thoughts and ways of God. Each aspect of the CompassionateCare Model can show signs of being broken.

- Our **feelings** may manifest brokenness in any of the following ways:
  - *Suppression of emotion.*
  - *Denial of emotion.*
  - *Projection of emotion.*

- *Emotions that are uncontained and out of control.*
- *Emotions that are guided by fear, guilt, shame, pride, greed, etc.*
- *Emotions that are driven by selfish desires.*

■ The brokenness of the **reasoning mind** may be manifested through:

- *Justifying irrational thoughts, feelings, or actions.*
- *Embracing self-centered thinking.*
- *Closing the mind to new ideas.*
- *Cutting off curiosity and the urge to explore.*
- *Taking direction from a self-imposed order, rather than God's order.*
- *Entertaining thoughts of temporal pleasure.*
- *Lacking humility.*
- *Harboring thoughts that originate in darkness.*

■ The brokenness of the **intuitive mind** may be manifested by:

- *Failure to open and develop.*
- *Failure to pray and reflect.*
- *Failure to recognize the possibility of union with God.*
- *Directing the intuitive mind toward fantasy and magical thinking.*
- *Allowing the imagination to be open to selfishness, and disordered passions that support: self-glorification, earthly fear, or wickedness.*

- A broken **will** leads us to:
  - *Make unhealthy choices that are driven by fear, pride, shame, guilt, greed, selfishness, or other signs of human weakness.*
  - *To know only our will or the will of others, ignoring God's will.*

As we grow in **Physical Wholeness** – holiness – our thoughts and ways move closer to the thoughts and ways of God.

- Our **feeling center** responds by making the following changes:
  - *Feelings are acknowledged and honored as psychic motors that stir us up and prepare us to act.*
  - *Feelings become manageable and they are used in healthy ways.*
  - *We learn to experience the desire to act without acting impulsively.*
  - *We are able to restrain our feelings and wait patiently for a sign to act.*
  - *We learn to offer our feelings to God.*
  - *We learn to sort our feelings by using the reasoning mind.*
  - *We can allow ourselves to get "stirred up" when it is time to act.*
  - *We cultivate healthy curiosity and allow it to move us toward appropriate exploration.*

■ Our **reasoning mind** responds by making the following changes:

- *Recognizing irrational thoughts and attempting to control them.*
- *Recognizing the common good, and moving beyond the self.*
- *Focusing on minimizing selfish thoughts.*
- *Using rational thinking to sort and control feeling impulses.*
- *Participating in a joint effort to use the reasoning mind and the intuitive mind in union with the feeling center to make good, healthy choices.*
- *Recognizing the need for continued growth and healing.*
- *Employing mental discipline.*

■ Our **intuitive mind** responds by making the following changes:

- *Beginning to open and develop through the grace to appreciate beauty and goodness.*
- *Learning to use reflection and meditation as a means to grow closer to God.*
- *Recognizing and beginning to use the capacity to envision.*
- *Realizing that oneness with God is possible.*

■ Our **will** responds by making the following changes:

- *We learn to make healthy choices.*
- *Our choices are guided by a desire to attain or maintain the common good and live in peace and harmony with a sense of internal well-being.*

Beyond physical wholeness we can grow toward **Spiritual Wholeness**. Growth in spiritual wholeness leads to union with God and greater fullness of life in Him.

■ As we grow in our relationship with God, our **feeling center** expands in the following ways:

- *We establish patterns of healthy intimacy.*
- *We have the capacity to bond with others and reach out to them in love.*
- *We learn to depend on God, not on ourselves or others.*
- *We engage in regular communication with God because of the desire to know Him.*
- *Filled with wonder and awe, we praise God.*
- *Because of the grace to appreciate beauty and goodness, we thank God.*
- *Feelings of humility and contrition fill our hearts.*
- *Our desire is to do what is pleasing to God.*
- *In tune with piety and devotion, we desire obedience to God.*
- *We learn to recognize God's presence.*
- *We find joy in our suffering because it brings us closer to Christ.*
- *We resonate with the truth.*

- The **reasoning mind** expands in the following ways:
  - *We put on the mind of Christ.*
  - *We are set free from a desire for temporal things.*
  - *We are released more and more from dark thoughts that imprison the mind and cause us to respond based on fear, pride, selfishness, etc.*
  - *We recognize and embrace the divine order.*
  - *We seek the truth.*
  - *We focus on the knowledge of God's word.*
  - *Our decisions are based on reason guided by faith.*
  - *We are attuned to God's thoughts.*
  - *We accept human dignity and through that reality find oneness with God and neighbor.*
  - *We learn what it means to worship in truth.*

- The **intuitive mind** expands in the following ways:
  - *Because we are growing in innocence and purity of heart our eyes are opened and we see God.*
  - *We are open to the promptings of the indwelling Spirit.*
  - *Life is a prayer.*
  - *Prayer and reflection are sources of conversion.*
  - *We learn to see from an eternal perspective.*
  - *We taste and see the goodness of the Lord.*
  - *Communion with God initiates healing of body, mind, emotions, soul, and will.*
  - *Hope springs eternal.*
  - *We learn what it means to worship in spirit.*

■ The **will** expands in the following ways:

- *We are attuned to God's ways.*
- *We desire to do God's will above all things.*

During our journey through life we will find ourselves to be broken in many ways. Some of us will have the courage to heal on a physical level. Others will even be motivated to move toward spiritual wholeness. The choice is always ours. God offers us the opportunity and provides us with the means to achieve healing. That healing process begins with faith – faith in God and faith in Jesus Christ. He calls us all to walk by faith. As a loving Father, He reaches out to each one of us on our journey with a desire in His heart for us to acknowledge the gifts He has given us for the journey – our feelings, our reasoning mind, our intuitive mind, and our will. How will you use the gifts that have been given to you by the Father?

May God bless you on your journey.

The Divine Praises

Blessed be God.
Blessed be His holy name.
Blessed be Jesus Christ, true God and true Man.
Blessed be the name of Jesus.
Blessed be His most Sacred Heart.
Blessed be His most Precious Blood.
Blessed be Jesus in the most holy Sacrament of the altar.
Blessed be the Holy Spirit, the Paraclete.
Blessed be the great mother of God, Mary most holy.
Blessed be her holy and immaculate conception.
Blessed be her glorious assumption.
Blessed be the name of Mary, virgin and mother.
Blessed be St. Joseph, her most chaste spouse.
Blessed be God in His angels and in His saints.

Guide to the Appendix

Appendix

The following prayers were written for those who practice the Catholic faith. At the same time, they have universal appeal for those who are called to follow Christ. If you are Protestant, please allow yourself to *move beyond* any words that might present obstacles to your Protestant thinking, and attempt to *embrace* the essence of the prayer.

An Act of Faith

O my God, I firmly believe that you are one God in three Divine Persons, Father, Son, and Holy Spirit. I believe that your Divine Son became man, and died for our sins, and that He will come to judge the living and the dead. I believe these and all the truths which the Holy Catholic Church teaches, because you have revealed them, who can neither deceive nor be deceived.

An Act of Hope

O my God, relying on your almighty power and infinite mercy and promises, I hope to obtain pardon of my sins, the help of your grace, and life everlasting, through the merits of Jesus Christ, my Lord and Redeemer.

An Act of Charity

O my God, I love you above all things, with my whole heart and soul, because you are all-good and worthy of all love. I love my neighbor as myself for the love of you. I forgive all who have injured me, and I ask pardon of all whom I have injured.

An Act of Contrition

O my God, I am heartily sorry for having offended you, and I detest all my sins, because I dread the loss of Heaven and the pains of Hell, but most of all because they offend you, my God, who are all-good and deserving of all my love. I firmly resolve, with the help of your grace, to confess my sins, to do penance and to amend my life.

Devotions to the Holy Spirit

Seven Prayers to the Holy Spirit

A Prayer for Purity

Most sweet Holy Spirit, true fountain of all grace, who
on the holy day of Pentecost did so perfectly purify the
hearts of the apostles from all sin, by the fire of the divine
love, that they were prepared to become an ornate dwell-
ing place for You; I ask that You purify my poor heart
through Your grace, that it may appear quite pure before
the eyes of God. Amen.

A Prayer for Union with God

Most benign Holy Ghost, who on the holy day of Pentecost did melt the hearts of the apostles in the fire of Your
divine love so that their hearts flowed into the heart of God
and were received in His image; I humbly ask to receive
this same fire of Your love so that my heart may be entirely freed from all earthly thoughts and that I may be
converted to God, becoming entirely united with Him.
Amen.

A Prayer for Strength in Adversity

O Holy Ghost, most rich in love, who on the holy day of
Pentecost did so inflame the hearts of the apostles that they
– who had been timid and weak and full of self-love – be-

came so strong and steadfast that they did not even fear death, but rather saw it as a joy and an honor to them to suffer shame and disgrace for God's sake; I pray that Your love might strengthen me against all evil and make me steadfast in all good, enabling me to patiently suffer hardships and accept them joyfully. Amen.

A Prayer for Self-Denial

Most charitable Holy Spirit, who on the holy day of Pentecost did lavishly fill the hearts of the apostles with the wine of divine love that they, being inebriated with love, forgot themselves and desired neither honor nor advantage for themselves, but sought only the honor and glory of God in all things. I pray that You inebriate my soul with the wine of divine love as You did for the first apostles, causing me to deny honor and possessions for myself, and inspiring me to seek the honor and glory of God in all things. Amen.

A Prayer for Heavenly Sweetness

O most brilliant Holy Ghost, who on the holy day of Pentecost did so richly penetrate the hearts of the apostles with heavenly sweetness that from that time forward no human consolation could turn them away from God; I pray that You fill my heart with heavenly sweetness causing it to transcend earthly joy and find my delight in things that are eternal. Amen.

A Prayer for Charity

O most tender and gentle Holy Spirit, who on the holy day of Pentecost did take possession of the hearts of the apostles and inspire them with love for heavenly things, causing them to experience inexpressible love of God and preparing them to go to Him through a thousand deaths; I pray that You inflame my heart in such a manner with love for divine and heavenly things that from my whole heart I may desire God alone and esteem death with all its pains as nothing. Amen.

A Prayer for the Gifts of the Spirit

O ever-blessed Holy Ghost, who on the holy day of Pentecost did with Your seven gifts so arm and enrich the hearts of the apostles that they appeared before God and the angles in the highest beauty and decoration; I pray that Your seven gifts will adorn my soul like seven precious stones and convert what is now defaced and deformed by sin into a vision that will appear beautiful and perfect in the eyes of God. Amen.

Litany of the Holy Spirit
(for private devotion only)

Lord, have mercy on us.
Christ, have mercy on us.
Christ, hear us.
Christ, graciously hear us.

Response: Have mercy on us.

God, the Father of Heaven,
God, the Son, Redeemer of the world,
God, the Holy Ghost,
Holy Trinity, One God,
Holy Ghost, who proceeds from the Father and the Son,
Holy Ghost, co-equal with the Father and the Son,
Promise of the Father,
Gift of the most high God,
Author of all good,
Consuming fire,
Burning love,
Spiritual healing,
Spirit of truth and of power,
Spirit of wisdom and of understanding,
Spirit of counsel and of fortitude,
Spirit of knowledge and of piety,
Spirit of the fear of the Lord,
Spirit of remorse and of penance,
Spirit of grace and of prayer,
Spirit of charity, peace and joy,
Spirit of patience, perseverance and goodness,
Spirit of gentleness, mildness and fidelity,
Spirit of self-control, chastity and modesty,

Holy Ghost, the comforter,
Holy Ghost, the sanctifier,
Who, in the beginning did move upon the waters,
By whose inspiration spoke the holy people of God,
Who did overshadow Mary,
Who did cooperate in the miraculous conception of the
    Son of God,
Who did descend upon Him at His baptism,
Who, on the day of Pentecost did appear in fiery
    tongues,
By whom we are also born again,
Who dwells in us,
Who governs the church,
Who fills the whole world,
Holy Ghost, *we beseech Thee, hear us.*

Response: *We beseech Thee, hear us.*

That You would inflame our hearts with the fire
    of Your love,
That You would impart to us Your heavenly graces,
That You would enlighten us with Your holy
    inspirations,
That You would lead us in the way of Your
    commandments,
That You Yourself would be our everlasting reward.

Lamb of God who takes away the sins of the world,
    spare us, O Lord!
Lamb of God who takes away the sins of the world,
    graciously hear us, O Lord!
Lamb of God who takes away the sins of the world,
    have mercy on us, O Lord!

Verse: Create in us a clean heart, O God,
Response: *And renew a right spirit within us.*

Let us pray

Grant, O merciful Father that Your divine Spirit may enlighten, inflame and cleanse our hearts; that It may penetrate us with Its heavenly fear, and make us fruitful in good works. Through Christ, our Lord. Amen.

Adapted from: Key of Heaven: a prayerbook for Catholics. *W.H. Litho Co. New York. 1973.*

Devotions to the Precious Blood

*Realize that you were delivered from the futile way of life
your fathers handed on to you,
not by any diminishable sum of silver or gold,
but by Christ's Blood beyond all price. (1 Pt. 1:18-19)*

Novena Prayer

Jesus, Man of Sorrows, accept the homage I wish to render Your most Precious Blood during this novena, as a token of my sincerest appreciation for the sorrows and sufferings You have willingly borne to atone for my many sins and to prove how much you love me.

I adore You as my very God, Who willed to become Man in order to save me from eternal death.

I thank You as the best Friend I have, Who laid down Your life as proof of the greatest love possible.

I ask pardon for having so little thought of You, the Man of Sorrows, and for having caused Your sorrows and sufferings by the many sins I have committed.

I pray to You, good Jesus, for all the graces I need to know You, to love You and serve You faithfully until death, and to save my soul. Give me a fervent devotion to Your Sacred Passion by which I was redeemed, venerating especially Your Precious Blood. Teach me how to unite the sorrows and sufferings of my life with Your own.

Through the merits of Your most Precious Blood and the prayers of Your Mother of Sorrows, I ask for this special favor: (*Mention your request*).

With childlike trust I abandon myself to Your holy Will concerning my request. If it should not please You to grant what I ask, I beg You, give me that which You know will be of greater benefit to my soul.

Grant me the grace to know You, to love You, and to be truly sorry that I have offended You. I ask this grace by Your Precious Blood:

By that Precious Blood which bathed Your Sacred Body and trickled down to the ground in the Garden of Olives.

By that Precious Blood which poured forth from Your Body during the scourging.

By that Precious Blood which covered Your Sacred Face when You were crowned with thorns.

By that Precious Blood which burst forth from Your hands and feet on Calvary.

By that Precious Blood which came forth from Your Sacred Heart after Your death.

By that Precious Blood which is still offered daily on our altars at Holy Mass.

By that Precious Blood which we drink in Holy Communion and of which You said, "He who feeds on My Flesh and drinks My Blood has life eternal."

Offering

Eternal Father, I offer You the most Precious Blood of Jesus Christ in atonement for my sins, in supplication for the holy souls in purgatory, and for the needs of holy Church.

Eternal Father, I offer You the most Precious Blood of Jesus with all its merits:

To expiate all the sins I have committed during all my life.

To purify all the good I have done poorly.

To supply for the good I ought to have done, and that I have neglected all my life.

Prayer

Almighty and Eternal God, You have appointed Your only-begotten Son as the Redeemer of the world, and willed to be appeased by His Blood. Grant, we beg of You, that we may worthily adore this Price of our salvation, and through Its power be protected from the evils of this present life, so that we may rejoice in its fruits forever in heaven.

Lord Jesus Christ, You came down from heaven to earth from the bosom of the Father and shed Your Precious Blood for the remission of our sins. We humbly beg of You that in the day of judgment we, standing at Your right hand, may deserve to hear: "Come, you blessed," for You live and reign forever. Amen.

Litany to the Precious Blood

Lord, have mercy.
Christ, have mercy.
Lord, have mercy.
Christ, hear us.
Christ, graciously hear us.
God, the Father of Heaven, *have mercy on us.*
God, the Son, Redeemer of the world, *have mercy on us.*
God, the Holy Spirit, *have mercy on us.*
Holy Trinity, One God, *have mercy on us.*
Blood of Christ, only-begotten Son of the Eternal
Father, *save us.*
Blood of Christ, Incarnate Word of God, *save us.*
Blood of Christ, of the New and Eternal Testament,
save us.
Blood of Christ, falling upon the earth in the Agony,
save us.
Blood of Christ, shed profusely in the Scourging,
save us.
Blood of Christ, flowing forth in the Crowning with
Thorns, *save us.*
Blood of Christ, poured out on the Cross, *save us.*
Blood of Christ, price of our salvation, *save us.*
Blood of Christ, without which there is no forgiveness,
save us.
Blood of Christ, Eucharistic drink and refreshment
of souls, *save us.*
Blood of Christ, stream of mercy, *save us.*
Blood of Christ, Victor over demons, *save us.*
Blood of Christ, courage of Martyrs, *save us.*
Blood of Christ, strength of Confessors, *save us.*
Blood of Christ, bringing forth Virgins, *save us.*

Blood of Christ, help of those in peril, *save us.*
Blood of Christ, relief of the burdened, *save us.*
Blood of Christ, solace in sorrow, *save us.*
Blood of Christ, hope of the penitent, *save us.*
Blood of Christ, consolation of the dying, *save us.*
Blood of Christ, peace and tenderness of hearts, *save us.*
Blood of Christ, pledge of eternal life, *save us.*
Blood of Christ, freeing souls from purgatory, *save us.*
Blood of Christ, most worthy of all honor, *save us.*
Lamb of God, You take away the sins of the world:
   spare us, O Lord.
Lamb of God, You take away the sins of the world:
   graciously hear us, O Lord.
Lamb of God, You take away the sins of the world:
   have mercy on us.

Verse: You have redeemed us, O Lord, in Your Blood.

Response: *And made us, for our God, a kingdom.*

Let us pray

Almighty and Eternal God, You willed to honor the standard of the life-giving Cross by the Precious Blood of Your only-begotten Son. Grant, we beg You, that they who rejoice in honoring the same holy Cross and His Precious Blood may rejoice also in Your ever-present protection. We ask this through the same Christ our Lord. Amen.

Found in: Treasury of Novenas. *Catholic Book Publishing Co. New York. 1986.*

Devotions to the Sacred Heart

Promises for First Friday Devotions

The promises of Our Lord to Saint Margaret Mary in favor of those who are devoted to His Sacred Heart.

1. I will give them all the graces necessary in their state of life.
2. I will establish peace in their houses.
3. I will comfort them in all their afflictions.
4. I will be their secure refuge during life and, above all, in death.
5. I will bestow a large blessing upon all their undertakings.
6. Sinners shall find in my Heart the source and the infinite ocean of mercy.
7. Tepid souls shall grow fervent.
8. Fervent souls shall quickly mount to high perfection.
9. I will bless every place where a picture of My Heart shall be set up and honored.
10. I will give to Priests the gift of touching the most hardened hearts.
11. Those who shall promote this devotion shall have their names written in My Heart, never to be blotted out.

12. I promise you in the excessive mercy of My Heart
    that My all-powerful love will grant to all those who
    communicate on the first Friday of nine consecutive
    months the grace of final penitence; they shall not
    die in My displeasure not without receiving the
    Sacraments; My Divine Heart shall be their safe
    refuge in this last moment.

An Act of Reparation
to the Sacred Heart of Jesus

O sweet Jesus, Whose overflowing charity for men is
requited by so much forgetfulness, negligence and con-
tempt, behold us prostrate before your altar eager to re-
pair by a special act of homage the cruel indifference and
injuries, to which Your loving Heart is everywhere subject.
Mindful alas! That we ourselves have had a share in such
great indignities, which we now deplore from the depths
of our hearts, we humbly ask Your pardon and declare
our readiness to atone by voluntary expiation not only for
our own personal offenses, but also for the sins of those,
who, straying far from the path of salvation, refuse in their
obstinate infidelity to follow You, their Shepherd and
Leader, or, renouncing the vows of their baptism, have cast
off the sweet yoke of Your Law.

We are now resolved to expiate each and every deplor-
able outrage committed against You; we are determined
to make amends for the manifold offenses against Christian modesty in unbecoming dress and behavior, for all
the foul seductions laid to ensnare the feet of the innocent,
for the frequent violation of Sundays and holidays, and
the shocking blasphemies uttered against You and Your
Saints.

We wish to make amends for the insults to which Your Vicar on earth and Your priests are subjected, for the profanation, by conscious neglect or terrible acts of sacrilege, of the very Sacrament of Your divine love; and lastly for the public crimes of nations who resist the rights and teaching authority of the Church which You have founded.

Would, O divine Jesus, we were able to wash away such abominations with our blood. We now offer, in reparation for these violations of Your divine honor, the satisfaction You once made to Your eternal Father on the cross and which You continue to renew daily on our altars; we offer it in union with the acts of atonement of Your Virgin Mother and all the Saints and of the pious faithful on earth; and we sincerely promise to make recompense, as far as we can with the help of Your grace, for all the neglect of Your great love and for the sins we and others have committed in the past.

Henceforth we will live a life of unwavering faith, of purity of conduct, of perfect observance of the precepts of the gospel and especially that of charity. We promise to the best of our power to prevent others from offending You and to bring as many as possible to follow You.

O loving Jesus, through the intercession of the Blessed Virgin Mary, our model in reparation, deign to receive the voluntary offering we make of this act of expiation; and by the crowning gift of perseverance keep us faithful unto death in our duty and the allegiance we owe to You, so that we may all one day come to that happy home, where You with the Father and the Holy Spirit live and reign, God, world without end. Amen.

I Will Not Leave You Orphans

Form of Consecration
to the Most Sacred Heart of Jesus

O most Sweet Jesus, Redeemer of the Human race; behold us prostrate most humbly before Your altar. To You we belong; Yours we wish to be; and that we may be united to You more closely, we dedicate ourselves each one of us today to Your most Sacred Heart.

Many have never known You; many, despising Your command, have rejected You. Have mercy on them all, most merciful Jesus, and draw them to Your Sacred Heart. Be You King, O Lord, not only over the faithful who never have gone away from You, but also over the prodigal children who have forsaken You; and make them return quickly to their Father's house, lest they perish of misery and hunger. Be You King of those who have been misled by error, or separated by schism; and call them back to the haven of truth and the unity of faith, so that there may soon be one fold and one Shepherd.

Grant to Your Church, O Lord, assurance of freedom and immunity from harm; give peace and order to all nations, and grant that, over the whole earth, from pole to pole, may resound the words: Praise to the Divine Heart, through which was brought to us salvation; glory and honor be to It forever. Amen.

O Heart of love, I put all my trust in You; for I fear all things from my own weakness, but I hope for all things from Your goodness.

Most sweet Heart of Jesus, grant that peace, the fruit of justice and charity, may reign throughout the world.

Sacred Heart of Jesus, protect our families.

188

Litany of the Sacred Heart

Lord, have mercy on us.
Christ, have mercy on us.
Lord, have mercy on us.
Christ, hear us.
Christ, *graciously hear us.*
God the Father of heaven, *have mercy on us.*
God the Son, Redeemer of the world, *have mercy on us.*
God the Holy Spirit, *have mercy on us.*
Holy Trinity one God, *have mercy on us.*
Heart of Jesus, Son of the Eternal Father, *have mercy on us.*
Heart of Jesus, formed by the Holy Spirit
    in the womb of the Virgin Mother, *have mercy on us.*
Heart of Jesus, united substantially with
    the word of God, *have mercy on us.*
Heart of Jesus, of infinite majesty, *have mercy on us.*
Heart of Jesus, holy temple of God, *have mercy on us.*
Heart of Jesus, tabernacle of the Most High,
    have mercy on us.
Heart of Jesus, house of God and gate of Heaven,
    have mercy on us.
Heart of Jesus, glowing furnace of charity,
    have mercy on us.
Heart of Jesus, vessel of justice and love,
    have mercy on us.
Heart of Jesus, full of goodness and love,
    have mercy on us.
Heart of Jesus, abyss of all virtues, *have mercy on us.*
Heart of Jesus, most worthy of all praise,
    have mercy on us.

Heart of Jesus, King and center of all hearts,
have mercy on us.
Heart of Jesus, in which are all the treasures of wisdom
and knowledge, *have mercy on us.*
Heart of Jesus, in which dwells all the fullness of the
Divinity, *have mercy on us.*
Heart of Jesus, in which the Father is well pleased,
have mercy on us.
Heart of Jesus, of whose fullness we have all received,
have mercy on us.
Heart of Jesus, desire of the eternal hills,
have mercy on us.
Heart of Jesus, patient and rich in mercy,
have mercy on us.
Heart of Jesus, rich to all who invoke You,
have mercy on us.
Heart of Jesus, font of life and holiness,
have mercy on us.
Heart of Jesus, propitiation for our sins,
have mercy on us.
Heart of Jesus, saturated with revilings,
have mercy on us.
Heart of Jesus, crushed for our iniquities,
have mercy on us.
Heart of Jesus, made obedient unto death,
have mercy on us.
Heart of Jesus, pierced with a lance, *have mercy on us.*
Heart of Jesus, source of all consolation,
have mercy on us.
Heart of Jesus, our life and resurrection,
have mercy on us.
Heart of Jesus, our peace and reconciliation,
have mercy on us.

Heart of Jesus, victim of our sins, *have mercy on us.*
Heart of Jesus, salvation of all those who hope in You,
    have mercy on us.
Heart of Jesus, hope of those who die in You,
    have mercy on us.
Heart of Jesus, delight of all the Saints, *have mercy on us.*

Lamb of God, You take away the sins of the world,
    spare us, O Lord.
Lamb of God, You take away the sins of the world,
    graciously hear us, O Lord.
Lamb of God, You take away the sins of the world,
    have mercy on us.

Verse: Jesus, meek and humble of heart.

Response: *Make our hearts like unto Thine.*

Let us Pray

Almighty and everlasting God, graciously regard the heart
of Your well-beloved Son and the acts of praise and satisfaction which He renders You on behalf of us sinners, and
through their merit grant pardon to us who implore Your
mercy in the name of the same Jesus Christ, Your Son,
who lives and reigns with You and the Holy Spirit, God
world without end. Amen.

Short Invocations

Jesus, meek and humble of Heart,
Make our hearts like unto Thine.

O Heart of Jesus, burning with love for us,
Inflame our hearts with love for You.

O Sacred Heart of Jesus,
May You be known, loved and imitated.

O Heart of my dear Redeemer,
May the love of Your friends make amends
For all the neglects which You sustain.

Let us, with Mary Immaculate,
Adore, thank, pray to and console,
The most sacred and well-beloved Eucharistic Heart of
   Jesus.

Found in: Key of Heaven: a prayerbook for Catholics. *W.H. Litho Co. New York. 1973.*

Process for Accomplishing Goals

The following pages describe a ten-step process that effectively integrates periods of action and reflection as they are used to move toward a goal or desired outcome. The best desired outcome is one in which God's will is known and pursued. This is accomplished through the cooperation between God's grace and human effort. In order to achieve the desired outcome there are steps to follow and choices to make. During each phase of the process we have the opportunity to remain open to God's inspiration and take action based on His will. This choice is presented in the Balance column for each phase which is described on the following pages. Those who strive toward communion with God and obedience to His will are familiar with this way of being.

However, God has given us the freedom to choose, and often we fail to choose Him. Instead, we choose to follow our own will. Sometimes our will causes us to do too much, and sometimes it causes us to do too little. In the chart on the next page, the left column (Deficient) describes those who do too little, while the right column (Excess) describes those who do too much. Only when we live in harmony with God's will can we find the balance that moves us forward guided by His grace.

As you review the steps of the process, notice which steps are familiar to you and which steps are foreign. Think about the process you follow when you need to accomplish a goal. As you consider each step, notice whether or not you are centered (balanced) in your approach. See if you follow a pattern of doing too much or too little. Use the process as a self-assessment to discover how you move toward accomplishing a goal. Notice how effective your current process is and notice ways in which you could improve.

Aspects of the Process

1. Prayer Phase

A seed of awareness causes you to pray for discernment and clarity in God's will.

Deficient	Balance	Excess
Failure to pray. (Instead you move forward according to your own will.)	*Allow appropriate time for prayer and reflection, remaining open to God's inspiration and desiring His outcome rather than your own.*	Get absorbed in prayer and fail to act. OR Prayer is focused exclusively or largely on achieving your desired outcome.

2. Preparation Phase

You acknowledge the task that lies ahead, and seek a time of preparation during which you will be made ready to move forward.

Deficient	Balance	Excess
No awareness of a need for preparation.	*Appropriate awareness of preparation.*	Excessive awareness of preparation phase/dwelling on it without doing anything.

3. Prayer Phase

You feel that you have been made ready through both your efforts and God's grace. You pray for discernment regarding the appropriate time and manner to begin.

Deficient	Balance	**Excess**
Failure to pray.	*Prayer that leads to appropriate action.*	Pray without acting.

4. Initiation Phase

Things seem to come together and draw you toward beginning the task at hand.

Deficient	Balance	Excess
Failure to initiate.	*Appropriate initiation.*	Excessive initiation (Begin too many things based on your own will).

5. Prayer Phase

You recognize that this process requires effort and work on your part. You pray for guidance, strength, endurance and perseverance.

Deficient	Balance	Excess
Failure to pray.	*Prayer that leads to appropriate action.*	Pray without acting.

6. Follow Through Phase

You recognize that the work has begun, and that it requires you to monitor and guide the process toward closure.

Deficient	Balance	Excess
Failure to follow through.	*Appropriate follow through.*	Excessive follow-up. (Dwelling on details and demonstrating a lack of trust).

7. Prayer Phase

You realize that work naturally evolves toward a satisfactory conclusion. It is important to recognize and accept completion of the work. In this phase you maintain a prayerful attitude about completion of the work, and you look forward to the phase of rest and appreciation that follows completion.

Deficient	Balance	Excess
Failure to pray.	*Prayer that leads to appropriate closure and resting.*	Pray without acting.

8. Closure Phase

You have the grace to bring the task to satisfactory conclusion.

Deficient	Balance	Excess
Failure to bring closure.	*Appropriate resolution and closure.*	Inappropriate or poorly-timed closure. (Closure driven by your will rather than God's).

9. Resting Phase

You recognize the need to rest after your efforts.

Deficient	Balance	Excess
Failure to rest and enjoy what has been accomplished.	*Appropriate time spent resting and appreciating.*	Excessive dwelling in resting (becoming lazy).

10. Prayer Phase

You realize that the purpose of your work is as a steward of God's creation, and that you must offer praise and thanks to Him.

Deficient	Balance	Excess
Failure to pray in thanksgiving.	*Appropriate prayer.*	Misguided prayer and feelings of self-glorification.

This ten-step process can be used in a conscious way to proceed toward a goal that has been set in the present or it can be used to reflect on the process you have used in the past. In either case the process has the capacity to provide self-knowledge. It is important to notice which phases you use and which phases you tend to omit. It is also important to recognize how you respond during each phase of the process. Do you tend to focus intensely on some phases, doing too much? Do you lightly pass over phases, doing too little? It is enlightening to notice the patterns you have developed as you pass through the phases.

You may also spend time reflecting on what prompts you to act. Are you motivated to act because of authentic love – love of God, self, and neighbor? Or are your actions prompted by selfishness, fear, guilt, shame, need for approval, or some other source of motivation?

The purpose of describing the process is to provide a sequence of steps that keep you ever-mindful of including God in all that you do and including Him in your life. It will also help you begin to integrate prayer and reflection into your daily life. If you use this process regularly, self-discovery will become a way of life for you. As a result of adopting this process you will grow in your relationship with God and in your life as an authentic Christian.

Stations of the Cross

By His Wounds You Are Healed

Introduction

All aspects of life have a beginning, a middle, and an ending. This is true for our development as Christians. Our life as authentic Christians begins with an awakening. Somehow we come to understand that life can be different. Often the awakening process causes us to be overcome with zeal. We recognize the goodness and kindness of Jesus, and we want to be just like Him. However, we are not yet prepared to follow in His footsteps. We are infants, and we have much to learn before we are ready to truly follow the Master. We learn these things one step at a time through growth in wisdom.

This set of Stations was designed to help Christians who are young in their faith learn to recognize some of the pitfalls that occur along the path of discipleship. Rather than walking the Way of the Cross with Jesus, this set of Stations allows the reader to follow Jesus in His passion, while resting in the arms of God the Father.

These Stations contain new insights and seeds of wisdom that can benefit Christians who are just beginning to walk with Christ. They can also help Christians who have difficulty accepting the reality of suffering as part of the journey.

Preface

People were bringing even infants to Him
that He might touch them, and when the
disciples saw this, they rebuked them.
Jesus, however, called the children
to Himself and said, "Let the
children come to Me and do not prevent
them; for the kingdom of God belongs
to such as these. Amen, I say to you,
whoever does not accept the kingdom of God
like a child will not enter it." (Lk. 18:15-17)

As you prepare to enter into the healing process offered by this version of the Stations of the Cross, allow yourself to recall the experiences of your childhood. Recall also the times when you have been touched by the innocence and blessedness of children in your midst.

Recall the essence of childhood – a childhood that is as yet untainted by the harsh realities of this world. Recall and experience the delight of watching a butterfly in a meadow. Recall and experience the curiosity of watching squirrels gather nuts for the winter. Recall and experience the wonder and awe of watching waves crash to the shore and advance on the sandy beach. Recall and experience the exuberance of the first winter snowfall. Recall and experience the great sense of joy and anticipation as you awaited a visit with your most treasured companion – whether it was mom, dad, grandpa, grandma, aunt, uncle, cousin or friend.

As you re-experience such events, they should create images in your mind, feelings in your heart, and notice-

able changes in your physiology. Allow the most vivid
memory to settle in your mind. ... Experience the feelings
that are associated with this memory. ... Allow the thoughts
and the feelings to physiologically enliven your body with
the sensations of joy, anticipation, delight, wonder, awe,
and excitement. Remain in this state of awareness as Jesus
shares with you the story of how much He loves you. Let
us walk with Him now through the Stations of the Cross
and listen to His story.

I The First Station
Jesus is Condemned to Death

V. We adore You, O Christ, and we praise You.

R. Because by Your Holy Cross You have redeemed the world.

Think of Me as your best friend – someone you love and someone who loves you in return. Some people are about to hurt Me badly and put Me to death. You love Me and you'd like to protect Me, but you can't. It's hard for you to stand by and watch Me as I am condemned to death. It's hard to imagine that any good can come as a result of suffering and death. Part of you wants to make it stop. Part of you wants to run and hide. Part of you feels numb and can't respond at all. Most of all, you feel confused and afraid. What should you do? When you face difficult, painful, even insurmountable challenges or obstacles in your life, you should always pray first. Pray just as I have taught you, saying:

Father, hallowed be Your name,
Your kingdom come,
Give us each day our daily bread
And forgive us our sins
For we ourselves forgive everyone in debt to us,
And do not subject us to the final test. (Lk. 11:2-4)

Pause now and wait for the Father to come to your aid.

Pause and reflect.

11 The Second Station
Jesus Embraces His Cross

V. We adore You, O Christ, and we praise You.

R. Because by Your Holy Cross You have redeemed the world.

The Way of the Cross is a difficult path to walk. It is especially difficult to walk alone. Remember that I said: "I will not leave you orphans; I will come to you." (Jn.14:18). Since you are young and just learning to walk this difficult Way of the Cross, stretch your arms up toward your Father in heaven that He might pick you up and carry you, until you learn to walk on your own beside Me. As I embrace My cross, feel My Father's loving arms embrace you.

Rest in His arms as He prepares you to witness the story of My love for you and My desire to see you reconciled to our Father.

Pause and reflect.

III The Third Station
Jesus Falls the First Time

V. We adore You, O Christ, and we praise You.

R. Because by Your Holy Cross You have redeemed the world.

It is difficult for you to see how I am burdened by the weight of the cross. You want to withdraw as you watch the soldiers beat Me and speak harshly to Me. Your heart is wrenching as you witness the extent of My suffering. You cannot bear it. As I fall, you bury your face in our Father's chest. He provides comfort and consolation for you.

Rest in His arms, and find healing and strength.

Pause and reflect.

IV The Fourth Station
Jesus Meets His Sorrowful Mother

V. We adore You, O Christ, and we praise You.

R. Because by Your Holy Cross You have redeemed the world.

The Father's strength has given you the courage to continue the journey with Me. However, you are confused. How can such a kind and loving God allow this horrible suffering to occur for His Beloved Son? You feel the strength of His love for Me, just as you have begun to experience the strength of His love for you. Your heart seeks wisdom and understanding in this time of confusion. The Father explains: "This is the wisdom of the cross – the wisdom that is known and shared by those who are capable of authentic love. This wisdom lives in the heart of Mary, the mother of Jesus. It can dwell in your heart, too, when you seek the truth and live in imitation of her. Notice how she offers loving support to her Son as He carries out My will."

Rest in the arms of God now. Ask for the grace to say "yes" to His will, and the dedication to live it in imitation of Jesus and Mary.

Pause and reflect.

V The Fifth Station
Simon Helps Jesus Carry His Cross

V. We adore You, O Christ, and we praise You.

R. Because by Your Holy Cross You have redeemed the world.

The strength of conviction is beginning to resonate within you now. You have the courage to unite with Me more intimately in My journey. You are able to open your eyes and witness My struggle without turning away. The Father continues to give you strength as His grace allows your eyes to open and see more clearly. The road is long and the struggle is difficult. You are beginning to feel the strength that God's grace gives you in these times. The same strength that gives Me the courage to move forward is now infusing you. You begin to experience the grace of perseverance and fortitude. You begin to understand how I can keep moving forward. Lean your heart against the heart of our Father and experience the outpouring of His love – the love that sustains Me from within. The strength of His love is not haughty and prideful. It does not cause Me to move forward with self-righteousness and the attitude that: "I can do it myself." Rather, this is a love that upholds union and cooperation. It is a love that helps Me to recognize when I am in need of help from others. It is a love that is filled with gratitude for the service and the assistance of Simon, my brother.

Rest comfortably in our Father's arms, and come to know this strong and humble love.

Pause and reflect.

VI The Sixth Station
Veronica Wipes the Face of Jesus

V. We adore You, O Christ, and we praise You.

R. Because by Your Holy Cross You have redeemed the world.

Strong and humble love can make you bold in your faith. Veronica gives us an example of bold faith. In her love, she has the courage to come to Me in this time of persecution. She has no fear of being harmed herself. She is not offended by the circumstances of My suffering. She does not turn away from Me, repulsed by the guilt and shame that surround Me. Her love is strong enough to move beyond these emotional obstacles. Her love brings her to My side, where she tenderly wipes My Face. Her compassion gives comfort and consolation to My Sacred Heart.

Rest your heart against the heart of our Father, and share the joy He feels when His children show compassion for others.

Pause and reflect.

VII The Seventh Station
Jesus Falls the Second Time

V. We adore You, O Christ, and we praise You.

R. Because by Your Holy Cross You have redeemed the world.

As you see Me fall the second time, you struggle to be free from our Father's arms to come to My aid. Gently, you are restrained. You are still in the learning phase and not yet prepared to assist others. Learning to wait and be patient are gifts that come with maturity. When you are ready, you will be prompted by God through the Spirit, and the path will be made known to you. For now, focus on the process of formation.

Rest in the arms of our Father, and ask to be more deeply attuned to His will for you.

Pause and reflect.

VIII The Eighth Station
Jesus Meets the Holy Women of Jerusalem

V. We adore You, O Christ, and we praise You.

R. Because by Your Holy Cross You have redeemed the world.

Watch Me closely in this Station as I move beyond the pain and suffering of the cross to speak words of wisdom to others. This type of action can only come through emotional, intellectual, and spiritual maturity. This requires time and guidance. It is wisdom that brings life and understanding. Seek *her* that you might authentically serve Me.

Rest in the bosom of wisdom.

Pause and reflect.

IX The Ninth Station
Jesus Falls the Third Time

V. We adore You, O Christ, and we praise You.

R. Because by Your Holy Cross You have redeemed the world.

Growth in wisdom gives purpose and meaning to life. It is a lifelong process – a developmental process. Just as you struggled to walk as a young child, so, too, will you struggle to learn wisdom. There will be times when you pull yourself up and race forward with strength and exuberance. There will also be times when you trip and fall. It's all part of the process of development. Through the mystery of the Incarnation I have given honor to all stages of the developmental process. As a toddler, I struggled to walk and, at times, I fell. Unite your struggles to Mine. Recall how close your Father in heaven is to you in this moment. The closeness of this relationship will guide you as you walk, and pick you up when you fall.

Rest now in the loving arms of the One who is the Author of this process and delights in all aspects of it.

Pause and reflect.

X The Tenth Station
Jesus Is Stripped of His Garments

V. We adore You, O Christ, and we praise You.

R. Because by Your Holy Cross You have redeemed the world.

As you grow in wisdom, you grow in union with God. This growth involves both "holding on" and "letting go." Through the spirit of discernment you learn to "hold on" to the things that are eternal, and "let go" of the passing things of this world. Letting go can be difficult. You have become attached to your old patterns, even though you know they are obstacles to greater union with God. Come to Me in this Station when you find it difficult to let go of your weaknesses and failings. Just as My garments are now being stripped away from Me, I will give you the grace to allow your affection for sin to be stripped from you. By My wounds you are healed.

Rest in the grace of a Father who heals the wounds of His children.

Pause and reflect.

XI The Eleventh Station
    Jesus is Nailed to the Cross

V. We adore You, O Christ, and we praise You.

R. Because by Your Holy Cross You have redeemed the world.

The pain of these nails creates the wounds in My flesh - wounds through which you are healed. Pray now: "Jesus, hide me within Your wounds. Never let me be separated from You."

Rest in our Father's embrace as you experience being hidden in My wounds and united to Me through them.

Pause and reflect.

XII The Twelfth Station
Jesus Dies on the Cross

V. We adore You, O Christ, and we praise You.

R. Because by Your Holy Cross You have redeemed the world.

Growth comes through the process of death and re-birth. Recognize what needs to die in you, so that you may be born again in Me – born from above. The process of dying and rising will re-fashion you in My image. See yourself as the *beloved one of God*.

Rest in His arms as His beloved child.

Pause and reflect.

XIII 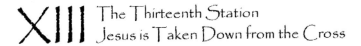 The Thirteenth Station
Jesus is Taken Down from the Cross

V. We adore You, O Christ, and we praise You.

R. Because by Your Holy Cross You have redeemed the world.

I am taken down from the cross by those who love Me. They tend My wounds – the wounds which are the source of your healing and growth.

Rest now in the arms of your Father as He tends your wounds.

Pause and reflect.

XIV The Fourteenth Station
Jesus is Laid in the Holy Sepulcher

V. We adore You, O Christ, and we praise You.

R. Because by Your Holy Cross You have redeemed the world.

Healing takes time. Preparation for re-birth and resurrection takes time. The time of rest in the sepulcher prepared Me to rise on the third day.

Rest with Me here and be prepared to rise with Me.

Pause and reflect.

Walking in Grace
– a meditation –

This is a meditation to facilitate walking in grace. ...
Find yourself a comfortable position, either seated or
lying down. ... Make sure it is a position in which you
can remain alert and attentive to my voice. ... The
objective is for you to follow my voice as it leads you in
your meditative experience. ...

Begin by breathing gently. ... Inhale and exhale. ...
Allow the breath to come in and cleanse your mind,...
your body,... your emotions,... and your soul... Breathe
in peace and relaxation. ... As you exhale, let go of any
concerns or worries, anxieties or fears. ... Continue
breathing gently. ...

Now allow yourself in some way to experience the
presence of Christ. ... *(Pause)* Breathe in the peace that
is offered to you through Christ. ... Exhale and let go of
anything that prevents you from fully accepting the
peace of Christ. ... *(Pause)* Experience the breath as
something which enlivens you and provides life-giving
energy for your journey . ... The breath is a direct gift to
you from God. ... Feel the breath of life as it enters your

body… the breath of life that is the power of God's
Spirit. …

Acknowledge that there are two aspects of you that
are in opposition. … You have an active part and a
reflective part. … See them as opposites and allow them
to be connected by an infinity sign with one flowing into
the other. … Feel the part of you that is active and
responsible for moving in the world. … Now feel the part
of you that is receptive and reflective. … Experience the
flow as you move from activity to receptivity and back
again. … This time, as you flow from the phase of activity into receptivity… allow yourself to pause in the
reflective state and come more into the fullness of the
receptive aspect of who you are. …

In this reflective place… allow yourself to be touched
by the gift of docility that comes from the Spirit
of God. … Allow that gift to bring forth and enliven the
truth of the feminine nature within you. … Experience
the fullness of this feminine nature. … Invite the Spirit to
resonate with the qualities in you that allow you to be
receptive to the will of God. … *(Pause)* Imagine yourself
as an open vessel — a vessel that receives enlightenment,
… promptings, … and inspiration from the will of God

through the power of His Spirit. ... Feel the sense of safety... security... strength... and love that come to you as you *receive* from God. ...*(Pause)*

Now allow yourself to become aware of how open and free-flowing God's gift of grace is to you. ... Know that the grace of God is always flowing in an outward direction from God to you. ... Are you allowing yourself to receive the fullness of His grace? ... Experience a stream of water as something that depicts the flow of God's grace as it comes toward you. ... What is that stream like for you?... Is it open... direct... and unobstructed? ... Are there winding turns?... Are there places where it is very wide and open? ... Are there places where it becomes narrow?... Is the path free and clear?... Does your stream have rocks that restrict the flow of water – the flow of God's divine grace to you?... *(Pause)*

If the path appears to be obstructed... ask for an understanding of what is obstructing this path of grace. ... *(Pause)* Invite those things that are obstructing your path to be moved aside or taken away. ... *(Pause)* Ask now to receive the flowing gift of God's grace in the way that God would have you receive this grace. ... *(Pause)*

Notice now how you receive God's grace. ... Are you like a container that gathers the flow of divine grace, allowing it to touch and heal you?... Or do you allow God's grace to flow through you and out into the world? ... Invite Christ to be your light of discernment and help you know when you need to be a container and hold onto God's grace. ... versus when you need to be a conduit and dispense God's grace. ...What is God calling you to do now?... Allow yourself to be guided by His will. ...

Now allow yourself to move beyond the level of your conscious awareness and into the place created by the underlying rhythm of creation. ... Ask God to allow you to touch that underlying rhythm in a very special way. ... Experience the underlying rhythm of creation. ... Begin to move with it. ... Experience the influence of divine grace as the Source of movement for that underlying rhythm. ... Experience what it is like to *go with the flow*. ... *(Pause)*

Invite the Lord to teach you how to touch this underlying rhythm in your daily life. ... If there are things that you need to add to your daily life to help bring forth a conscious awareness of this rhythm, invite them to come into your life and awareness now. ... If there are things that are preventing you from touching this underlying rhythm each day, offer them up to God. ... Ask to be released from them so that this underlying rhythm becomes an important part of your life. ...

Invite this rhythm to become like an underground spring that will bubble up to eternal life and restore you each and every day. ... Feel the underlying rhythm that is God's grace in the earth. ... Feel the stream that flows from this rhythm. ... Experience the spring as it bubbles up within you. ... Allow it to be your source of grounding and connection to the earth. ... *(Pause)* Feel the heavenly flow of divine grace that comes from the heart of God as it enters you. ... Allow that to be your connection to the heavens. ... *(Pause)*

Experience yourself now as an open vessel connecting heaven and earth. ... as a vessel that is prepared by the gift of God's grace to move forward in this life. ... encountering with confidence each of the things on your path toward perfection. ... Feel the gift of humble confidence that prepares you to move forward on your path. ...

As you prepare to return to the present moment. ... gather all of the positive effects of your meditative experience today. … Know that God is releasing you from anything that might prevent you from having and holding the experience you have been given today. … Take time now to give thanks for grace you have experienced. … Ask God to prepare you to return to full conscious awareness … ready to undertake your work in this world. …

Wiggle your fingers and toes to enliven your circulation. … Stretch. … Slowly and gently open your eyes and enter the present moment.

Bibliography

Blamires, H. (1963). *The Christian mind: how should a Christian think?* Ann Arbor, MI: Servant Publications.

Colson, C. & Pearcy, N. (1999). *How now shall we live?* Wheaton, IL: Tyndale House Publications, Inc.

Dubois, J. (Ed.). (1995). *The nature and tasks of a personalist psychology.* New York: University Press of America, Inc.

Hackney, H. & Cormier, L.S. (2001). *The professional counselor: a process guide to helping* (4th Ed.). Boston: Allyn & Bacon.

Jones, S. & Butman, R. (1991). *Modern psychotherapies.* Downers Grove, IL: Intervarsity Press.

Koenig, H. (1999). *The healing power of faith: how belief and prayer can help you triumph over disease.* New York: Simon & Schuster.

Vitz, P. (1977). *Psychology as religion: the cult of self-worship.* Grand Rapids, MI: William B. Eerdsman Publishing Co.

ST. JOSEPH INSTITUTE

About the Institute

The primary mission of St. Joseph Institute is to heal and to teach, according to the grace offered by God and in alignment with His holy will. Toward that end we offer retreats and individual sessions that present instruction based on the Gospel message, and provide opportunities for guests to heal in all aspects of their humanity, striving always to grow in the image of Christ.

Our facility is located in the mountains of Central Pennsylvania, midway between Altoona and State College. The campus features beautiful log and stone buildings sited on 62.5 acres. Gardens, walking trails, recreation areas and a children's playground surround the chapel, three lodges and the Laurel Wellness Center.

The Institute welcomes businesses and organizations for meetings and training programs; families, couples and individuals for vacations and get-away weekends; church groups of all denominations for retreats; and guests of the wellness center who are seeking renewal and healing. More than 40 treatments are available – ranging from therapeutic massage to Christian counseling. The Institute also offers retreats and training programs on topics that include healing, spiritual growth and relationship skills.

For additional copies of this book, contact the Institute or visit our website (www.stjosephinstitute.com).

St. Joseph Institute
134 Jacobs Way
Port Matilda, PA 16870
814-692-4954